Lift Up Your Hands

Lift Up Your Hands

RAISE YOUR PRAISE AND
GET LOST IN GOD

GLORIA P. PRUETT

West Bloomfield, Michigan

WARNER BOOKS

NEW YORK   BOSTON

Published by Warner Books with Walk Worthy Press™

Warner Books

Time Warner Book Group
1271 Avenue of the Americas, New York, NY 10020

Walk Worthy Press
33290 West Fourteen Mile Road, #482, West Bloomfield, MI 48322

Visit our Web sites at www.twbookmark.com and www.walkworthypress.net.

Printed in the United States of America

First Edition: November 2005
10 9 8 7 6 5 4 3 2

Library of Congress Cataloging-in-Publication Data
Pruett, Gloria P.
    Lift up your hands : raise your praise and get lost in God / Gloria P. Pruett.—1st ed.
        p. cm.
    Summary: " 'The ABC's of Praise' as a simple and powerful tool to help readers focus and develop their personal praises during daily prayer time."—Provided by the publisher
    ISBN 0-446-57823-1
    1. Praise of God. 2. God—Worship and love. 3. Prayer—Christianity. I. Title.

BV4817.P78 2005
248.3—dc22   2005000386

I want to thank and dedicate this book to my children, Charles, Carlton, and Kelli, for their love, support, and encouragement as I endeavored to follow God. I love you so much. You have stuck by me and loved me unconditionally. Through the good and bad times, you always had a hug, hair-rub, smile, some witty comment that strengthened me, and, yes, at times some unsolicited advice. During the journey, you never pressured me for things but were satisfied and content to have my love. If I could have my pick of children, my choice would always be the same—the three I have—and for that I am a blessed woman!

Jesus wasn't stingy with His Blood . . . why should we be stingy with our praise?

ACKNOWLEDGMENTS

Writing acknowledgments has been very difficult. How do you summarize in a few pages all of the people who have helped you throughout the years? My greatest fear is leaving someone out. So, I say this up front: I cannot name everyone, and if I omit someone, please charge it to my head and not to my heart. So many people have contributed to my success in many different ways. Time and ink will not allow me to state individually what everyone has done; most of you would be embarrassed for me to put it on paper, because what you did, you did to bless me, not to have me put it in print. Please know that without you I could not have stepped out in ministry as I have done. You all have touched my life in your own unique and special way, and by listing your name, I am saying "thank you for your contribution." With that said, and before I acknowledge anyone else, I want to thank My Heavenly Father, the Lord Jesus Christ and Precious Holy Spirit. Words cannot express my love for Them, but perhaps this book will give you a glimpse of my feelings. Yes, *I* wrote the book, but it was Their idea and the Holy Spirit's continued direction and guidance that got the job done.

To my grandchildren, Carlton II (CJ) and Cariel: One look from you and I found strength to work three more hours. You've brought much joy to my life. Thanks also to their mom, Tosha Williams, and her dad, Joe Williams.

Next, I wish to thank my spiritual parents, Dr. Keith A. Butler, pastor of Word of Faith International Christian Center, and his wife, Minister Deborah L. Butler. They grew me up in the things of God and changed many dirty spiritual diapers. Had it not been for them, I don't know if I would be doing what I am doing today. I also want to honor their children, who are awesome anointed ministers as well: Co-Pastor Keith A. Butler II and his wife, Minister Tiffany Butler, and their daughter, Alexis Nichol Butler; Minister MiChelle A. Butler and Minister Kristina Butler.

I want to thank Nancy Libby and the girls, Arlene Reindel, and Annie and Harry Coakley. We've been friends and shared so much over the past twenty-something years. And for the past eight especially, you all have carried me, helping me to fulfill the call of ministry on my life, and you never once tired. Words cannot express my love for you. To Linda Ellis, my prayer partner, who stayed up hours with me to pray, encourage, research, and read. I thank God for our special bond. Thank you to your husband, Ken, who allowed you to be a blessing to me and your children. To Stacey Hanks, who would stop what she was doing and read just because I asked. To Carol Couch and mom, Mrs. Jordan, and Rhonda Wright, thanks for the home-cooked meals, which got me through some tough times. Thanks to Neal Wright for letting your wife, Rhonda, cook and for all the things you've fixed around my house. To Sylvia Powell and Ruby Ware: We've been friends for forty-six years—gracious!

To my most wonderful brothers and their wives: Oliver and family, Raymond and family, James and family, Malcolm and family, and

John and family. To the sweetest sisters: Denise and family, Jacqueline and family, and Brenda and family. To Uncle Carnell and Aunt Barbara and family. To my Aunt Willie Bowden (I know you're really my cousin) and family. To my cousin Charline and family. To my niece Vikki (Valesia), thanks for all your help. To my unique cousin Punkin (Claudette Trice): I can depend on you calling me at one o'clock in the morning just to say hi, bless your darling heart. And thank you to all of my cousins.

To some of my church family at large: I can't name you all, nor the many churches you represent, but for starters, Dr. Stanley L. Scott and his wife, Minister Carolyn Scott, thanks for getting me through two years of school and nurturing me many years later. To Pastor Raymond McClintock and his wife, Andrea, you're so special to me. To Minister Deborah Banks. To Minister Cheryl Gill, Minister Lois Vaughn and her husband Nathaniel (we can laugh at anything). To Minister Andrea Simpson (you made me write when God was trying to and I was disobedient), Minister Joy Gaddis, Evangelist Kathryn Stramler, Pastor Joel E. Gregory, Minister Linda Burdette, Evangelist Marie Diggs, Minister Lee Bell (we've had some wonderful after-hour talks), Minister Stephen Bell, Pastor Solomon and Minister LaVita Turner, his wife. To Ministers Derrick and Angela Greene: While visiting you in San Francisco this book was birthed. Angela, remember when you and I were walking by the water praying—what special moments and friendship! To Bishop George Davis and his wife, Minister April Davis; Bishop Kevin E. Wright and his wife, Minister Leslie Wright; Pastor Keith Echols and his wife, Minister Renee Echols. And to Minister Michelle Stramler. To all of the pastors of the Word of Faith Satellite Churches. To Darryl and Daisy Jones and Aaron Hightower, who came through for me big time at a low time in my life. To my praise instructors—this is how it all got started—Minister Doyle and Linda

Tucker; Willie (Mr. Mack) and Kym McAllister (thank you for giving me my first praise book); and to my praise buddies George and Rosetta Archer, Mark and LaTonya Jackson, Darlene and John Boswell, and Vanessa Davis. To Ajene and Felicia Maxwell, thanks for reading my contracts. To Minister Ronald Pritchett, who early on encouraged me to continue writing and spoke blessings over my life regarding publishing. You are truly special.

To Pastor Harail Johnson and his wife, Joan, along with Pastor Damon Green and his wife, Minister Cassandra Green: You mighty people of God lent me your precious books and gave me priceless advice when I went on the road to minister. Upon my return, you were always there with an open ear and suggestions for my next engagement. Thank you.

To Pastor Barbara Anthony, your husband, John, and the Mitcham Church A.M.E. family: You opened your pulpit and allowed me to feed your sheep on numerous occasions, and I'm honored. Your friendship means a lot. Mitcham family, I love you; Rev. Sharon Kennedy-Collins, my sista; Earl and Shirley McCullough and girls.

To Denise Stinson, I'll never forget what you told me at a conference: "If you must choose between writing and spending time with God, spend time with God." You are so special, thank you for everything.

To my editors, Irene Prokop and Susan Higgins: You are some awesome women, and I am so thankful for all you've done and the encouragement along the way. Your editorial skills amaze me! To Robert Castillo, managing editor of Warner Books, thanks for everything. And to the whole Time Warner Book Group and Walk Worthy Press, many thanks to you for making all of this possible and putting my dreams into print.

To my GM family: William J. and Leslie O'Neill, Tom and Chris

Pyden, Peg Holmes and Kari Nattrass and family. God used you to bless me while attending ministry school, and you're still blessing me even now. Thank you.

To my neighbors, who mowed the lawn, took out garbage, shoveled snow, fixed whatever, you know: Jerry and Val Gardner, Irvin and Sandra Mixon, Sharon McWilliams and her sons, Roy and Shirley Goodwin, Johnny and Rose Mitchell, and Janice Coleman and her girls. To the lovebirds Cordell and Donna Barker.

To William and DayDawn Butler and family (thirty-four years of friendship and still going), Pete and Daphne Adams, Janice Riddley, Stan and Carol Hill, Mary McDonald, Joyce Stephens, Lynette Flowers, Cliff and Brenda Jackson, Renee Greer, Marshall and Beatrice Johnson, LaTanya Terry, Jeannie Jackson, LeShell and Romel Arrington, Deborah White, Richard and Fern Baker, Morris and Marilyn Bell, Johnny and Patricia Carreker. To the Pruetts: Charles Sr. (Carol Rudledge), Charles Jr., Sandra, Caresse, Gwendolyn, Vanessa, Rickey, and Colleen. To Mrs. Andrea Ayler and the Westside Academy gang.

In loving memory of my dad Oliver, my mother Ethel, my grandmother Maggie, my uncle George, my brother-in-law Chole, my nephew Chris, Pastor Percy Gill, and Minister Jeff Davis.

There are many others I'd like to thank, but then that would be another book!

CONTENTS

CONTENTS

Allow Yourself to Experience Praise

Let every thing that hath breath praise the Lord. Praise ye the Lord.

PSALM 150:6

My grandmother was a pastor and, from the time I was in my mother's arms until now, I have always been in somebody's church forty-five (or more) Sundays of every year. I was taught many things: Live right and you'll please God; if you don't live right, God will punish you. And, depending on the church I attended, God's only directive seemed to be the Do Not's—do not do this, do not do that. But the subject of praise and how to do it never came up.

Around 1986, I joined a church where the pastor taught the Word of God directly from the Bible, and my life literally changed. Suddenly, I began to see things in the Bible that I had never seen before. I began to experience things that I had never experienced before, like praising God and praying in the Holy Spirit. As often as I attended church in the past, I had never felt nor was I taught these things. How sad not to be exposed to something so beautiful as praise!

I figure I have been offering praise to God for about twenty years, but the last ten have been the most heartfelt. What do I mean by that? I mean the praise that came from my lips was a deep, earnest sincere praise. Yet it saddens me that I have been a Christian for fifty-three years but have only been praising for twenty. What happened during the thirty-three years I missed? Was God not good to me the first thirty-three years? Had He done nothing in my life that warranted an expression of my gratitude in the form of a "thank you"? Didn't He deserve some sort of praise?

Because I was not taught to praise, it wasn't on my to-do list. This is not something I'm proud of, but I share it with you because I want you to know that even if you aren't praising God now, you can be. And if you are praising Him, you can use my "ABC's of Praise" to take your praise to the next level.

I have been called to share what I've learned about praise to help you *develop* and *enhance* your praise to God. I want your personal praise time, the time you spend at home or when you're alone praising God, to be so sweet and special that you will get "lost" in your praise and expressions of gratitude. You won't even know what time it is, you'll be so focused on your praise.

Our focus will be on your personal, intimate time at home or alone with God. If you learn to praise on your own at home, then the praise leader at church won't have to work so hard!

For those of you who aren't sure why you should praise at home besides the fact that the Bible tells us we should praise God, let's look at the following scenario:

A married couple is in a crowd. The husband is found holding his wife's hand, smiling and gazing into her eyes and saying all the right things. He even whispers sweet nothings in her ear. The crowd sees him and approves. "He's the man," they murmur, and they secretly admire him. However, as soon as this couple gets in their car and vanishes from the eyesight of others, the husband, who was so loving in front of the crowd, suddenly shuts down. He ceases to say nice things to his wife. He rarely looks at her. He totally ignores her until they are once again in the presence of other people. You can imagine how his wife must feel!

Well, God has feelings too! Don't you think He wonders why you praise Him in church but ignore Him when you're alone—just you and He—together? I'm not talking about the daily "Thank You for waking me up"; "Thank You for my job." How about stretching your hands in the air when you wake up in the morning and saying: "Heavenly Father, You've given me so much to be grateful for, let me just honor You before I do anything else. Good morning, Jesus, my Savior. How wonderful to get up and be in the presence of such Royal Guests. Holy Spirit, my treasured Friend, once again I can do the impossible because I have You as my hanging Buddy." That beats a cup of coffee first thing any day. Let's experience daily how sweet it is to declare continued praise to our God.

After reading this book, and implementing its concepts, you won't be a clock-watcher; you'll be a thinker. If you are a drifter during praise, you'll become challenged. Time will fly and you'll have fun telling God how you feel about Him. What a great place to be!

Once you begin to use my concept of the ABC's of Praise, your thoughts will quickly line up with your desire to shut out everybody and everything. You won't have to struggle because the concept will make you think only about God. You will no longer be a clock-watcher during prayer and praise.

When I began to focus on praise, I established various times for personal devotion. To this day I still have to fight for this because something always wants to steal the Lord's time from me. During devotion, I reserved a portion of time for praise, prayer, reading of the Word, and writing down my thoughts beginning with five minutes allotted for each. Eventually I increased my time. But I discovered the praise portion always got cheated and that bothered me. I was determined to do something about it.

Lack of time spent wasn't the only issue I had during my time of praise. I said all the "right things,"—"I love You, Lord." "I glorify Your Name." "I thank You for being Lord over my life." "Hallelujah, You deserve the highest praise." "I bless You, Lord"—all the traditional stuff. I did that for years until one day I came clean before God. I flat-out asked Him, "Don't You get tired of hearing me say the same things over and over?" I was tired of hearing myself. Was I expressing to God how I felt about Him at that moment? Or was I repeating what I had always said? I was in a rut. How did I *really* feel? Was I saying what was in my heart?

I finally asked Holy Spirit, "Please teach me how to love God with my whole heart. Help me to speak beyond my current vocabulary. Help me express to God on a daily basis what He means to me. Help me to not sound like a broken record, day in and day out. God deserves so much more from me. Help me, Holy Spirit, articulate to God and my Lord Jesus that I would be lost without Them."

When you cry out for help from your Helper, He will answer your prayers. When He answered me, the concept of this book began. Using the "ABC's of Praise" will get your mind and spirit to cooperate with each other for a common goal of uninterrupted, raw praise. No other outside thoughts (e.g., *What's for dinner? I've got to go to the cleaners! I don't believe he said that to me today!*) will dominate your time. You will successfully keep your mind and spirit solely on God as you enter and exit your praise.

Praise is a magnificent tool! Heartfelt praise is even more satisfying. Praise is a win-win situation. God gets the glory, and you leave His presence with a Kool-Aid™ smile on your face that no devil in hell can erase. Your life may still be the same as when you began to praise, but being in God's presence is a confidence builder. Now you can see yourself healed. You can sense your victory. You know you can win!

Sincere praise will erase depression and all your cares. You'll become lighter and feel as though you can conquer the world. But it takes more than two minutes. Praise is not something you do once a day along with your devotion. You may begin that way, but you won't continue that way. Praise is like prayer—it's a way of life, and, once you start it, you'll love it. As you begin to apply the principles in this book, you too will come to a place where you will get "lost in HIM." Come . . . let's grow in our praise.

Lift Up Your Hands

BLESS THE LORD

Bless the Lord, O my soul: and all that is within me, bless his holy name.

PSALM 103:1

Praise can be defined in many ways. It can mean to extol in words or song, to magnify, to glorify excellent works, or to express gratitude for personal favors or benefits received.

One Bible dictionary defines praise as: "One of humanity's many responses to God's revelation of Himself . . . Praise comes from a Latin word meaning 'value' or 'price.' Thus to give praise to God is to proclaim His merit or worth."

If you have seen any of God's excellent works or if you are grateful for anything God has done for you and you admire God, then you should praise Him. Scripture tells us that if we are breathing, we should praise.

We all like it when someone gives us praise. Everyone enjoys compliments. Suppose you finally bought a new suit with shoes and a purse to match? Your hair and makeup is fresh. You splurged and got the ultimate female combo (I'm not talking about a burger, fries, and a drink—I'm talking about the ultimate manicure and pedicure). You would have a fit if no one gave you a compliment at least once.

Men are no different: Your suit was made especially for you, your designer socks peek below the cuffs of your pants as you sit, and your 'gaters have the "boss gloss." Your tie and hanky are screaming along with your fresh hairstyle "look at me!" Tell me you don't swell when the compliments follow.

According to Genesis 1:26–27: *"And God said, Let us make man in our image, after our likeness: . . . So God created man in his own image, in the image of God created he him; male and female created he them."* If we are made in the image and likeness of God and we like praise, wouldn't it stand to reason that God Himself likes praise? Later as you read some of the scriptures herein, you will see that God not only likes praise, He *expects* it from us.

Remember this: Everything belongs to God. It all started with Him. Thus, if everything you own belongs to God—He's letting you use His stuff. It's only right to thank Him for using what's His. Psalm 24:1 says, *"The earth is the Lord's, and the fullness thereof; the world, and they that dwell therein."* This is repeated again in 1 Corinthians 10:26: *"For the earth is the Lord's and the fullness thereof."* Let's look at the same verse from the Amplified Bible: *"For the [whole] earth is the Lord's and everything that is in it."* Exodus 19:5(b) says: *". . . all the earth is mine."* Deuteronomy 10:14: *"Behold, the heaven and the heaven of heavens is the Lord's thy God, the earth also, with all that therein is."*

God owns everything—even the air you breathe. If God decided to cut off our oxygen right now, and I'm not talking about what's in a tube that can be purchased (that's His too), none of us would be able to live. We couldn't even breathe without God! I'm going to paraphrase a joke to illustrate my point.

> Several scientists went to God and told Him they figured out how to make a man without His help. Their man proved to be equal to the one He made. God's reply was *"Really?"* With a smirk on their faces and standing in a pool of arrogance—they replied "Really!" God then told them "Go ahead, let Me see what you can do." They began to pull their resources from a trunk, starting with a wad of dirt. God interrupted—took the dirt and politely said, "Get your own dirt—this belongs to Me."

You see, everything belongs to God. It's our duty and our privilege to praise Him!

When I spend time in God's presence, I feel like I can make it. I feel like *somebody*. My earthly situation before praise may be the same as it is after praise, but being in God's presence affects me in a positive way. The Word of God will have that same effect on you. You will be enlightened. You will read something several times and suddenly Holy Spirit will give you a new revelation that you never saw before. After reading His promises, you will experience hope that you never felt before.

Praise has one condition, however. If you want to feel good about what you're saying, then you need to have a personal relationship with God.

What if I said, "What a beautiful suit you had on last week," yet I didn't see you last week. You might respond by saying "I don't own a suit and I've never worn one." Wouldn't I feel dumb? I was trying to give you praise when I really didn't know you. If I really knew you, then I would have known that you didn't own a suit. Don't continue trying to praise God because of what you heard someone else say. Get to know Him and praise Him because of what you know about Him and what will make you lift up your hands in praise.

God's Word tells us what He expects from us. His Word describes His character and it tells us about Him as a Person. It tells us what He's done for us and what we can expect Him to do in the future. When you take time to read God's Word, and realize what He's done for you, you're better equipped to give Him the praise He deserves. You can accurately thank Him from the bottom of your heart.

The Bible, coupled with your life history, will give you all you need to know to praise God. We all have much to praise God for—our families, the predicaments He's gotten us out of, His mercy regarding our thoughts alone.

Reflect on your thoughts for a moment. God's forgiveness from your thoughts alone ought to cause you to extend your hands in praise. I know my thoughts and I know I'm not alone! I'm talking about vile, ugly thoughts. Clearly, God knows every thought that comes to your mind. Matthew 9:4 says: *"And Jesus knowing their thoughts said, 'Wherefore think ye evil in your hearts?'"* Matthew 12:25 reads: *"And Jesus knew their thoughts, . . ."*

You cannot allow your thoughts to run wild with sin. If the enemy brings you a thought and you cast it down, you have no problem with God. If you take that thought and begin to meditate on it, however, turning it over and over in your mind, that thought now becomes *yours* and not the devil's. You've taken that small thought and composed many thoughts from it. We need to do what 2 Corinthians 10:5 says: *"Casting down imaginations, and every high thing that exalteth itself against the knowledge of God, and bringing into captivity every thought to the obedience of Christ."* When a thought comes that is not of God, our responsibility is to "cast it down," not salivate and take possession of it.

I'm not just talking about those lustful and evil things that you know come from the enemy. I'm talking about the ones you've conjured up as well. Some of you have murdered more people in your thoughts than the serial killers who are locked up in prison. Some of you have gone to bed with more men and women than decency allows. And some of you have beaten your mother-in-law in your thoughts just this past week. The poor woman was lying on the ground bleeding and you continued to beat her in your thoughts. How many times have you strangled your boss in your mind? Too many to number! I'm making this comical because it goes down a little easier, but it's true.

These thoughts alone could land you in hell, but God through His mercy and grace keeps you. If you can't think of any reasons to praise God—*praise Him for not putting you in hell for your thoughts!* Proverbs 23:7 clearly says, *"For as he thinketh in his heart, so is he."* Unchecked thoughts will produce—good or bad! So watch your thoughts.

Let's lift our hands right now and say, "Thank You, Father, for having mercy on me and my thoughts. Thank You for not condemning me when I meditate on things that I know are not pleasing in Your sight. I'll honor You in my thoughts. From this day forward I'll be careful and cast down anything in my thought life that's not pleasing to You."

You should praise God for everything, but you will have trouble praising someone you don't know. You can only go so far and then you're stuck. For example, what if your mother bought you three dresses: one black, one blue, and one brown. You could begin to shower praises on her for being so nice, so thoughtful, so caring. You could think of many things to say to your mother to thank her for those dresses and her generosity. You might even say, "Mom, thank

GLORIA P. PRUETT

you for blessing me with these three dresses. You're the best mother in the world!"

But what if someone blessed you with three dresses and the gift was anonymous? Your praise would change. You could give praise for the gift, but you wouldn't know *who* to praise. This is what happens when you really don't know God. You believe the tangible things you acquire are a result of something you did. You paid your money for your clothes. You went to school and you deserved the promotion you got. But look at Psalm 75:6–7: *"For promotion cometh neither from the east, nor from the west, nor from the south . . . But God is the judge: he putteth down one, and setteth up another."* 1 Samuel 2:7 also says something similar to this . . . *"The Lord maketh poor, and maketh rich: he bringeth low and lifteth up."*

If you didn't know it before, you know now from Scripture that God owns everything. He is the Boss. Surely He deserves our praise.

CONVERSE WITH HIM

Enter into his gates with thanksgiving, and into his courts with praise: be thankful unto him, and bless his name.

PSALM 100:4

You can't talk to someone you don't know and you can't praise someone you don't talk to. God knows you—get to know Him.

I can't take for granted that everyone reading this book understands that God wants us to talk to Him. Consider these scriptures: 1 John 1:3: *"That which we have seen and heard declare we unto you, that ye also may have fellowship with us: and truly our fellowship is with the Father, and with his Son Jesus Christ. . . ."* 1 Chronicles 16:11 says: *"Seek the LORD and his strength, seek his face continually . . ."* John 15:16 tells us: *"Ye have not chosen me, but I have chosen you, and ordained you, that ye should go and bring forth fruit, and that your fruit should remain: that whatsoever ye shall ask of the Father in my name, he may give it you."*

These Bible references refer to fellowship, seeking God and asking Him for things. We need to ask God to help us develop good attitudes, godly character, integrity, patience, peace, and so forth. We've become proficient at asking for money, cars, and houses and yes, He wants us to have those things. But we need character builders first so we can handle the other blessings.

As a child I never talked to God. I thought God only talked to adults and ministers. But if you don't talk to Him, you certainly can't be praising Him like you should. I believed my grandmother talked to God for me. After all, she was a pastor and God always talks to pastors—never to people—or so I thought!

These childhood experiences with God remind me of a little girl I once saw at a baby shower. The adults were conversing with one another and it was obvious, once you noticed her, that she was in deep conversation with someone. As I looked closer I could tell she was discouraged. With her play cell phone in one hand and her other hand on her hips, mouth poked out—she was mad! It was really cute and I couldn't help but intrude. "Hi, honey, who are you talking to?" She looked at me, lowering her big brown eyes as she began to tell me that the person she was calling kept hanging up on her!

I couldn't help but chuckle on the inside because this precious baby really believed she was talking to a person on a toy cell phone and this person was choosing to hang up on her. I probed further. "Well, who were you talking to?" Without hesitation she said, "God!"

I couldn't control my laughter any longer. "Oh baby, God wouldn't hang up on you." She pushed the phone into my hand and said, "Um hum. Listen." I took the phone from her and pretended to talk with God.

"Hello, hello, God—yes, how are You? Well this little girl I'm looking at said You hung up on her. I didn't think so, hold on, here she is."

I handed the phone back to the little girl who now had a big smile on her face. Anxiously awaiting her turn to talk to God, brown eyes now bright and little hands waving as if to say "Hurry up and give it to me! I'm ready to talk to God." She was delighted we now had a connection!

With headset in place and a smile on her face she demanded, "God, why You keep hanging up on me?!" As quickly as the smile appeared it was gone. Her mouth returned to the pout, and her brown eyes dropped simultaneously with the phone as she spoke with a sigh—"He hung up again!"

Yep. That little girl was just like me! It always seemed as if God talked to the adults and Granny, but He didn't talk to us kids! As I got older, I realized that you don't need a phone to contact God when He's living inside of you!

If you've confessed Jesus as Lord of your life, He does live on the inside of you in the person of Holy Spirit. If you haven't confessed Jesus as Lord, you can wait until you finish reading this book, or turn to the "personal confession" section beginning on page 147 and you can be saved now!

Once I began to realize who God was and began to fellowship with Him, I discovered I didn't feel "comfortable" talking to Him. After all, why would the God who created the earth, made man, lived in heaven, and had angels bow down and worship Him at His throne talk to me? The idea was hard for me to comprehend. I was thinking too much and not reading enough of my Bible. The Bible is full of scriptures that tell about the love of God for you, how He wants to commune with you, that He expects praise from you as we discussed earlier.

If you aren't talking to God, He is talking to you. I know now that God talks to children *and* adults; they just confuse Him with their "conscious" and the "something told me" person . . . "You know . . .

something told me to call my son's teacher . . ." "Something told me to buy my wife some flowers." Stop calling Holy Spirit "something." Yes, there could be several voices talking to you at one time—the voice of God in the Person of Holy Spirit, your own voice, and the voice of the enemy. You need to know who's speaking to you! Attend a good Bible church and get information. Don't be like the little girl on the cell phone—God *is* talking to you. He's not hanging up on you. You just don't know how to listen.

The more you talk to God, the more you'll *want* to talk to Him. First, He's good at keeping secrets. He won't tell anyone else what you've said. After all, God sent Jesus to redeem you and Holy Spirit to live and dwell inside you to be your Best Friend. He will help you. Holy Spirit gives you life-changing insight. He'll give you a God idea.

During times of fellowship with God, I try to be very honest and straightforward with Him. Don't try to fool yourself or God. He knows your heart and what you're thinking. You can't continue to pretend that you're having a great time with Him when you're not. He's not like people. You can't fake it with Him.

Begin talking to God on a consistent basis and what a change in your life you'll see! Don't leave out Holy Spirit; He's a wonderful Friend who will talk to you at any time. Go ahead, put the book down and ask Him—"Is it true, will You talk to me now? Is it something You want to say?" Don't be a "chicken" as the adults used to tell me—do it and enjoy your Friend.

DARE TO KNOW ALL ABOUT GOD

My sheep hear my voice, and I know them, and they follow me:

JOHN 10:27

This particular scripture in my Bible is written in red, which means Jesus Himself spoke these words. He said we would know His voice and that He would know ours and we would follow Him. You get to know someone's voice if you hear it a lot, which means you must hang around them. My children can be in a crowd of people, but if they are talking I can pick them out. Many of you can do the same with your loved ones. You know your husband's voice, your wife's, and your friends. Hang around God long enough, talk to Him, and you'll know His voice.

After you start talking to God, you will get to know Him and His character. He's not the mean Ogre, as some of you were raised to believe. He's a Sweetie full of mercy and grace; a wonderful Savior to be respected and reverenced; God of glory, worthy of praise. He is the Holy One, our Anchor. He's faithful Father and Friend. As your Father, He can, and will, bring correction when needed.

Knowing God for yourself will help you praise Him. I remember praising God one day; I could feel His presence and it was oh so sweet. I was expressing to Him how good it felt to seek Him earnestly and verbalize what was in my heart. I began to sing a song taken from a wonderful Broadway musical *The King and I,* written by Rodgers and Hammerstein. The song is called "Getting to Know You."

I had a great time singing this song, even though I was singing the wrong words and making up my own. But because I felt the urge to serenade the Lord, I went on the Internet to find the correct words. When I found them, I began to dance and sing and jump around because I was so excited that I was "Getting to Know God" for myself. For once I was expressing my love to Him and the words were mine, all mine. There was nothing really "spiritual" about our time together. I was just happy being in His presence having Him all to myself.

God wants our hearts. He is not interested in us saying all the right things when in our hearts we're saying or feeling something else. Isaiah 29:13 in the Amplified Bible says: *"And the Lord said, Forasmuch as this people draw near Me with their mouth and honor Me with their lips but remove their hearts and minds far from Me, and their fear and reverence for Me are a commandment of men that is learned by repetition [without any thought as to the meaning]."* Wow, let's look at Matthew 15:8 in the Amplified as well: *"These people draw near Me with their mouths and honor Me with their lips, but their hearts hold off and are far away from Me."* Let's not be like the people referred to in these passages of Scripture. When we praise God, let it come from our heart and flow from our lips.

Did God care that the song I was singing to Him didn't come from a hymn book? I don't think so. I believe He had a smile on His face because I was praising and worshipping Him from my heart. Like a child, I was dancing before Him uninhibited by religion and other folks.

Perhaps your experience with God is much different from what mine used to be. I didn't even know if God *liked* me. When I was young, both in age and in the things of God, I knew He loved me, somehow; but you can love people and not like them or what they do. For example, if your fifteen-year-old goes shopping with you and decides to go down the clothing aisle and throw all the clothes on the floor, you wouldn't like your teenager at that moment. You'd still love the person but not the action.

I discovered that God not only liked me, He loved me. I found out I was the apple of His eye. I had been told so many lies about God earlier in my Christian walk. After reading the Bible for myself, I discovered that those things I had been told were misconstrued by me and the persons relating the information to me. God had been misrepresented. As you read about Him, talk to Him and fellowship with Him—praise Him. When you praise and love Him because you know Him for yourself, your praise will be true and from your heart.

When I was "getting to know God," I had a difficult time "cutting down all the weeds of religion." I felt like I was in a jungle cutting down bush. For example, people always told me what I couldn't do when serving God, but the Bible is full of can do's. They told me that God would strike me down, but I'm finding that He wants to lift me up. I've heard about God being the harsh Judge, but if you judge yourself you won't have to be judged by Him.

Ask yourself these questions: When was the last time you boasted about God? Which do you do more of—boasting, complaining, or asking? If you became an expert at praising God and fellowshipping with Holy Spirit, what would that do to your relationship with Him? Is He the subject you like most? Is He even close? Do you want to know about Him? What steps are you taking?

Do you really *like* God? Have you disliked God because someone told you your loved one died because God "needed another flower"?

God does not need to kill someone for another flower. If He can make a man and keep the sun in the sky, all He has to say is "flower be" and it will appear. God does not kill people for flowers or because He needs another angel.

If someone else hasn't shown you the Word of God, then get a Bible and read John 10:10: *"The thief* [satan] *cometh not, but for to steal, and to kill, and to destroy: I am come that they* [us] *might have life, and that they might have it more abundantly."* Another scripture (James 1:17) puts it this way: *"Every good gift and every perfect gift is from above, and cometh down from the Father of lights, with whom there is no variableness, neither shadow of turning."*

You can learn to like God—He's magnificent! John 3:16 tells us that God loves us so much that He gave His Son Jesus. *You don't do that for people you don't like!* And, you don't hang around people you don't like. Holy Spirit is your hanging Buddy; I'd say that He really likes you!

You want a good stress reliever? Try spending some time in the presence of God. The next time you find yourself praising God, before you leave His presence, ask Him—Lord, show or tell me something beautiful about You that I don't know—I really want to learn all I can. If He doesn't tell you right then, keep listening, keep looking around. He'll reveal something that you didn't previously know or see. No one can know all that there is to know about Him and we never will. He's too big. But if you're truly interested (and He'll know), He will share wonderful, beautiful things with you. Watch and see! He's done it for me and He'll do it for you!

Some of us may respect and fear God but don't feel we can say we love Him because we are afraid of God. We're scared that He is going to "get us" because of the thoughts and things we do that He doesn't like. That's why it used to be difficult for me to say, "I love You, Lord," and mean it from my heart. I said it—because it was expected. But what I *voiced* and *felt* were contrary to each other because I truly didn't know God.

Once I made a decision to get lost in my praise, I realized that I had a huge advantage. I had a Helper who not only knew God, but He is the Third Person of the Godhead—Holy Spirit! And help you He will, but you must be willing to talk with Him to find out how!

God has given us so many tools to help us study His Word and know all about Him. When reading His Word you will learn how He feels about you. And after you learn about Him all the days of your life, you still won't exhaust all that's in the Bible.

Like me, you too can sing the "Getting to Know You" song to God. God does not care that it came from *The King and I.* After all, in reality it's you and the King! You may come up with something wilder than that. Surely, when you get caught up praising God, the Holy Spirit will cause you to sing sweet songs of praise, and if you don't know a lot, you'll be surprised at what God will let you use to praise Him, once you dare to know Him.

ELEVATE YOUR PRAISE

Because thy loving kindness is better than life, my lips shall praise thee. Thus will I bless thee while I live: I will lift up my hands in thy name.

PSALM 63:3–4

Lift up your hands in the sanctuary, and bless the Lord.

PSALM 134:2

While I was vacationing in San Francisco, the Lord revealed to me that He wanted me to write this book. I awoke one morning and walked around the bay, praying and praising God. The scenery was picture-perfect. Surrounded by dancing water on both sides and lush greens, I felt God's presence like never before. The only sound was that of birds singing. I was thanking God for providing the resources for the vacation and praising Him for a job well done—palm trees swinging in the breeze, boats swimming in the bay, the wind gently embracing my skin.

Then, as usual, I began to praise God using what I call the "ABC's of Praise." I was thanking Holy Spirit for teaching me how to love God, when I heard Him whisper to me, "I want you to put this in a book." What a surprise to me! I then asked, "Put this in a book? Me? Why?" Holy Spirit then told me that "the personal experiences and concerns you have regarding praise are shared by others and they are seeking help as well in entering praise." It was further revealed that the principles I use to go to another level of praise will help those who truly want to "raise their praise" to God without being clock-watchers.

The Holy Spirit told me that in order to increase my praise I needed to pull out the dictionary and find words that expressed my love and gratitude to God. He said, "Begin with the letter *A* and go through *Z* declaring with each letter of the alphabet the goodness of God or my feelings about God." Holy Spirit challenged me to do it without the dictionary. Well, the first time was pretty easy. As I began to do it the second time the Holy Spirit said, "This time do not use any religious terms like Alpha and Omega, the Beginning and End, King of kings, Holy God, God of Mercy, God of Grace, God of Love, Hallelujah." It still wasn't too difficult until I got to the *Q, X, Y,* and *Z*. Those were the letters I got stuck on.

After about three or four times of doing this without the dictionary, I began to get stuck on other letters. Then the Holy Spirit said, "Now go to the dictionary and begin to write words from *A* to *Z* that you have not used to express how you feel about God." I got out a notebook and labeled the pages *A* through *Z*. As I scoured the dictionary I wrote words that expressed to me who God was and how I felt toward Him, His Son, and Holy Spirit.

Depending on your background you might be asking yourself, "Why does the author keep saying Holy Spirit said this and Holy Spirit said that?" When Jesus returned to heaven after rising from the dead, He didn't leave us to fend for ourselves. In John 14:16–17 Jesus says, *"And I will pray the Father and he shall give you another Comforter, that he may abide with you for ever. Even the Spirit of truth; whom the world cannot receive, because it seeth him not, neither knoweth him: but ye know him; for he dwelleth with you, and shall be in you."* John 14:26 says, *"But the Comforter, which is the Holy Ghost, whom the Father will send in my name, he shall teach you all things and bring all things to your remembrance, whatsoever I have said unto you."*

I want those of you who have confessed Jesus as Lord to know that you are blessed with the Person of Holy Spirit. He is your Comforter who is always with you because He lives inside you. He's a Teacher and Reminder. He will help you recall things. He's the Third Person of the Godhead. Holy Spirit should be so real to you that if you were by yourself and passed gas or belched, you would say, "Excuse me, Holy Spirit."

Once I realized Holy Spirit was a person, I started treating Him like one. The more you acknowledge Him and talk to Him, the greater the relationship.

Although this is not a teaching on Holy Spirit, you should know who you have on the inside. To me, praise is "loving on God" by telling Him "who He is to you." I didn't know how to do it naturally, but the Person who is always with me has known God since He was. What better Person to teach me how to love Him than someone Who's been with Him for eternity! And Holy Spirit will help you with your ABC's of Praise.

You will no longer continue, year after year, to say the same things to God. "Hallelujah, hallelujah, glory to God, glory to Your Name. I love You, Lord, I love You, Lord. You are good, You are good." Yes, God is all of these, but wouldn't you like to add something to that? He's too big, too wonderful, not to venture out and tell Him something different about Himself. Please don't misunderstand me—at times, especially during a worship service (or at home), you will still, even after practicing the ABC's of Praise, find yourself saying certain words or phrases over and over. It's okay to tell the Lord over and over how much you love Him. But find different ways to say it. He's a BIG God and we need to take the limits off our praise.

Go the extra mile for God and expand your praise vocabulary. When you do, wonderful things will begin to happen for you. Enlarge your praise tent. Write praise in the form of a letter. Or write Him a song or poem.

Buy a special notebook for praise and begin by spending maybe five minutes on each letter of the alphabet. After you write about ten words under each letter, begin to think about what you want to say to God. If it's on a day when everything is beautiful, then you might want to pen praise on how magnificent God is. Maybe it's not a good day— your check is gone and you haven't even touched the bills you need to pay; then your praise might be on the line of Jesus being your Provider. In the midst of this temporary lack, He's still worthy of praise. No matter how bad things seem, you can always find something to be thankful for if you truly desire to praise the Lord.

One day as I was praising God, I started with *A* and the word I used was "appreciate." I was telling the Lord how much I appreciated His faithfulness and in my spirit a light went on. I stopped in the middle of my praise and thought: How many words can I find that mean the same thing as "appreciate"?

I pulled out some of my resources (*Webster's Concise English Thesaurus* and *The Writer's Digest Flip Dictionary*) and this is what I found under **appreciate:**

> admire, adore, enjoy, esteem, gain, give thanks to, grateful, hold in high regard, increase, judge, like, love, recognize, respect, take pleasure in, thankful, treasure, understand, value, welcome.

I had a field day praising the Lord on that one word alone. I went crazy giving God praise. One word can become a whole praise when you go that extra mile. You will "raise your praise" by just using the word *appreciate*. Here's what I wrote:

Father, yes I **appreciate** You. Men *admire* many things but I have someone I can admire who won't let me down. That someone is You, Daddy. I admire the way Your Son in obedience went to the cross for me.

You're my hero, Jesus. I *adore* You and everything about You. I *enjoy* being in Your presence. Your company is sweet. I *esteem* You more than anything. I *gain* from being in Your presence. I gain strength, courage, peace. You name it, I gain it.

I *give thanks* to You for never quitting on me. I thank You for the precious Blood. I thank You for another day. I'm *grateful* for what You've done for me in spite of myself. I *hold in high regard* Your Word that changes my life. I *increase* in my spirit every time I'm in Your presence.

Judging from all I know about You, I would not want to live without You. You are Men of integrity. I *like* communing with You. I reap revelation, confidence, and encouragement when we hang out. I *love* You with all my heart, my soul, my very being.

I *recognize* that nobody, nowhere with the clout and status that You have would put up with me—but You. I *respect* everything about You. How You set standards and even abide by Your own standards.

I *take pleasure* in the fact of knowing that You don't operate on hearsay. You know me, You make Yourself available to me at all times. I take pleasure in knowing that You will never leave me. I'm so *thankful.* There are not enough words to express how thankful I am to You!

I *treasure* You more than silver, gold, or relationships. Those things are subject to change, but You will always be here with me. I *understand* what I've been blessed with. Having You as my Father, Jesus as my Lord and Big Brother, and Holy Spirit as my Friend, I need nothing else.

My *value* is increased just because I know You and because of the Name You've given me. The Name of Jesus! Every other name is below that Name and will bow to the Name of Jesus. I *welcome* You during this time of praise, because I know what I have in You! Glory to God!

I just wrote that from my heart using the word *appreciate.* How do you think our Father feels when His children take time to love Him like that! We're not in a hurry. We'll do whatever it takes to convey to Him with clarity how we feel. I think He'll be quite pleased.

As you can see, I started with one word—appreciate. The thesaurus rendered seventeen additional words and three phrases. Now log these words in your notebook for future praise under the correct letter. Each day, build on what you have. Not only did you receive one word for the letter *A* when you looked up that word in the thesaurus, you can now log all of the other seventeen words and three phrases we just talked about.

After you write your feelings on paper, and you're satisfied with the way it reads, go to the next step. Close the thesaurus and shut out any other thoughts. Stand and lift your hands and read your praise to the Lord out loud and boldly proclaim what you were able to pen after some thought. Be creative and spontaneous. Being free in your praise is wonderful and this is only the beginning.

I've already told you about my frustrations and inability to communicate my praise to God, but I had another issue as well: raising my hands. In the worship service, I lifted my hands to God like I was scared. My wrist was flipped up, so it gave the appearance that my hand was raised but my elbows were bent and clutching my side. One day, I looked around to see if anyone was watching me.

Let's look at hand-raising a little further. When you want to be heard in a crowded room, or get the attention of the person in charge, you don't yell and say "Hey, I want to talk." No, out of respect for their position, you raise your hand.

If you're in a fight and you decide to "surrender," you hold up your hands and begin to walk toward the one you're surrendering to. When you're at a sporting event and your team makes a great shot, or someone does something extraordinary, you stand up, thrust your hands in the air, and yell "Yeah!" Or you can lift your hands with clenched fists as a sign of "victory."

When I enter into the presence of the "One in charge of my life," out of respect to Him, I lift my hands. When I realize that I can't "fight the good fight of faith" without surrendering to God, I raise my hands in surrender. When I think about the winning team I'm on and all the extraordinary things that Jesus has done and is still doing, I lift my hands and say, "Yeah—You be the Man." When I come into the presence of the King, I honor Him by raising my hands in total awe of Who He is and the victory He has provided for me! Scripture tells us to come into the presence of the Lord lifting holy hands. So lift those holy hands unto the Lord!

During my transition from no praise to limited praise to where I am now, I remember an incident in the sanctuary that brought about another change regarding lifting my hands. I was lifting my arms during a praise song (I had not yet graduated to doing it at home), and my arms got tired after about half a minute into the song. They got so tired that I had to rest them by putting them down for a while. This bothered me. Here I was enjoying the praise, raising my arms and hands to the Lord, and my *flesh* made me put my hands down. I made a decision then that I would do something about it. If I decided to lower my hands during praise, it would be because I got a release in my spirit and not because of my flesh!

I immediately began to wonder how I could strengthen my arms so I could hold them up as long as *I* wanted to! One day while I was on my exercise bike, Holy Spirit told me to begin to "exercise my arms and strengthen them." What a revelation! You probably figured that out by yourself, but I needed help from my Helper.

I began to do arm exercises at home to build my arms. I wasn't exercising for me, I was exercising for the mission that nothing would hinder my praise. I was determined to go the extra mile in every area so I wouldn't be forced to lower my arms because I was tired. I bet Jesus was tired of having His arms stretched out on the cross, but He hung there determined to complete His assignment to redeem us. If Jesus could hang on the cross for my sins, surely I could keep my hands raised for the entire praise song *if I wanted to*! With arms extended to the side, I would begin moving my hands in a circular motion . . . 1, 2, 3, 4, 5, 6, 7, 8, 9, 10 . . . then I would repeat the cycle with my hands going in the reverse direction . . . 1, 2, 3, 4, 5, 6, 7, 8, 9, 10 . . . This was one complete cycle. I continued doing this until I had worked myself up to five cycles for a total of one hundred circles.

Next, I began to work on the horizontal motion. I extended my arms upward, palms facing the ceiling. Then, I would paddle my arms like riding a bike. I can't tell you how many of these I did, but I kept doing them until my arms were strengthened enough to hold them up as long as *I* wanted to! My flesh was not going to tell me, "You can put your hands down if you're tired, God will understand!" No! I would raise my hands to God until I felt released to let them down.

I'm not trying to tell you how long you should raise your hands to God—that's between you and God. But as you grow in your praise (and it takes time), you should increase in every area. I'm only sharing these things with you because again, if these were areas I struggled with, I know someone reading this book is feeling the same. I also know sharing what I went through will help you get delivered sooner than later.

However, if you don't feel comfortable in God's presence, your praise will not reach the level you desire. When I first began to praise, I didn't understand why God wanted me (a little nobody) to bestow accolades to Him. After discovering how much God loves me and that I am somebody because God said so, I understood why He wanted a relationship with me that included praise. I wanted to honor God. Jesus has made things so easy for us and I think sometimes we get too complacent with God. Because we have access to the Father, if we're not careful, our relationship becomes common. Instead of getting up for praying or praising, if it's cold with a lot of snow outside, we lie in the bed. I did it *once too often* and my Helper checked me. Holy Spirit said to me, "If the President walked into the room right now, would you lie in the bed and say, 'Hey, Mr. President.'?" No. If I knew the president was coming, I would get up, brush my teeth, comb my hair, and look like I was expecting royalty. Holy Spirit said, "You need to do that sometimes for the Lord—He's become too common to you." Wow, that jerked the slack out of me. Do I do this every time? No. But still at times I get on my knees before honoring and praising God. Sometimes I spruce myself up by combing my hair, dabbing on some perfume, and putting on something nice before ministering to God in the privacy of my home—why? Because He is God and He deserves my best.

Don't get so comfortable with God that you forget who He is. It's true He doesn't care how, or what, you look like, but if you dress up for your boyfriend or spouse, and God blessed you with them—dress up for Him sometimes too. Don't let the Lord remind you that the last time you were on your knees you were looking for a shoe under your bed. Get on your knees for Him. Then, with a smile on your face, hold up your arms while on your knees and say, "Lord, I bow before You today in honor and respect of Who You are. I just want to love You and give reverence on my knees."

If what I've just said agrees with your spirit, make sure you act on it.

THE FATHER IS WAITING JUST FOR YOU

I will sing unto the Lord as long as I live: I will sing praise to my God while I have my being.

PSALM 104:33

There are many ways to use the ABC's of Praise. Sometimes I'll use the same letter more than once. Don't limit yourself in how you use this principle. Be free to express to God how you feel. You can start by praying and just begin to praise Him. Start with *G* and go through *Z*. Or begin with *A* and go through *G*.

For your first try, do not use any of the praise language that you've used before (i.e., I love You, Lord; Glory, Hallelujah). Your praise won't be like mine, so don't try to put sentences together. Just say the letter of the alphabet and choose a corresponding praise. Keep your first one simple. Write down what comes to mind or use a dictionary if necessary. Remember, your word to the corresponding alphabet letter should remind you of the Lord and His faithfulness, His lovingkindness, and

His goodness. You can cheat by asking Holy Spirit to help you (smile). In the beginning always start with *A* and say something like this . . .

> Lord I stand before You, bursting with praise, and I want You to know that I **Applaud** You for the many times You've extended Your grace to me. Without You my life would be out of **Balance**. I praise You for being my **Champion**. I praise You for coming to my **Defense** when no one else would.

Before you begin to use the ABC's of Praise, I want you to confess what follows. It's not a praise, just a confession to build your confidence as you start your journey. I only used the ABC's of Praise format to write the confession. If you remember these twenty-six things (they will build your confidence), you will achieve your desire to "raise your praise and get lost in Him." You may need to refer back to them, so bookmark this page in advance. *Make sure you read the alphabet first, then what follows.*

> Father, when I think about "raising my praise and getting lost in You . . .

A   lets me know that You are **Approachable.**

B   assures me that I can **Build** on our relationship.

C   reminds me that You **Chose** me first.

D   lets me know that this will not be **Difficult.**

E   says that I'm going to **Enjoy** this!

F   tells me to not **Faint** in the process.

G   reminds me that my **Goal** is to **Grow** in praise!

H   says that **Holy Spirit** will help me learn to praise You.

I   will allow me to **Imagine** how wonderful You are.

J   declares the **Journey** will be sweet.

K   You are the **Key** to my success and You deserve the honor.

L   I won't **Limit** my resources in my quest to raise my praise.

M   I'll **Make** the adjustment to spend time to praise You.

N   I'll no longer be **Narrow** in my thinking.

O   You have **Opened** the door to great and wonderful things.

P   I'm going to **Proceed** with a vengeance!

Q   I won't **Quit** praising You—ever!

R   I **Refuse** to give up!

S   I'll no longer be **Satisfied** with my praise as it is now.

T   This is a new and **Thrilling** experience!

U   I'm expecting **Unusual** fellowship with You.

V   My praise will **Virtually** be revolutionized.

W   I **Want** so much for You to be pleased.

X   Your **X-ray** vision into my heart confirms my sincerity.

Y   I **Yearn** to go higher in my praise.

Z   I'm **Zany** about You and I'm not ashamed to say so.

If you remember what's written above, you will be successful in raising your praise.

It's your turn now. Go through the alphabet and think of ways to praise the Lord. I've already put the letters in place at the end of this section. If you need to, go to a dictionary, but be determined to get your praise on. If possible, try real hard to do it on your own the first couple of times, without help from outside sources. Let me warn you that *Q, V, X, Y,* and *Z* will take a lot of imagination, but you have Holy Spirit, your Helper. You'll be amazed at what He will teach you about loving God!

You will get better with practice. The best part is that while doing this, your thought life will be totally focused on the Lord. Go ahead, write your first ABC's of Praise and then don't forget to lift your hands after you write it and speak it out loud to the Lord.

A   =   _____

B   =   _____

C   =   _____

D   =   _____

E   =   _____

F   =   _____

G   =   _____

H   =   _____

I   =   _____

J   = _____

K   = _____

L   = _____

M   = _____

N   = _____

O   = _____

P   = _____

Q   = _____

R   = _____

S   = _____

T   = _____

U   = _____

V   = _____

W   = _____

X   = _____

Y   = _____

Z   = _____

Go ahead, try another one.

A   = _____

B   = _____

C   = _____

D   = _____

E   = _____

F = _____

G = _____

H = _____

I = _____

J = _____

K = _____

L = _____

M = _____

N = _____

O = _____

P = _____

Q = _____

R = _____

S = _____

T = _____

U = _____

V = _____

W = _____

X = _____

Y = _____

Z = _____

Very good!

GO FOR IT!

Let my mouth be filled with thy praise and with thy honor all the day.

PSALM 71:8

N ow that you've learned the ABC concept, let's write some more. I'm going to teach you various ways to praise; later you can add your own. I'll show you how to apply the ABC's of Praise using mostly *biblical terms*. Later, we'll do "strictly from the heart"; we'll get *r e a l* serious, and we can't and won't leave out a fun one. I'm even going to show you how to praise using negative circumstances—yeah! And you'll have more opportunities to write some. Remember: Our purpose is to think about God and all that He is, so much so that we aren't thinking about doing the dishes, cooking dinner, presenting a work project, cutting the grass, or shoveling the snow.

The ABC's of Praise, if done correctly, will again block out everything else that's vying for your attention so you can quickly "get lost in

Him." Let's begin by praising using familiar terms. Read the following praise from *A* to *Z*, then read it again really praising God as Holy Spirit prompts you.

Lord, I lift my hands to You today, to honor You and all that You are and for what You've done. The Atonement for my sins was enough, but You didn't stop there. You gave me Your written Word in the form of a Bible that feeds me spiritual food, nourishing my body. Calvary was not a pretty picture, but You went there anyway, just for me, where You bore every Disease so that I wouldn't have to. What an awesome God You are! Because of the cross, You made available to me Eternal Life. You're so wonderful. Your mercy and grace is infinite. You Forgive me when I sin and promised in Your Word that You would remove my transgressions as far as the east is from the west. You amaze me with Your patience.

Just thinking about You, my hands go up and I say "Glory." You are a Holy God and because of You I can be holy too. After all, I've been made in Your Image and Justified. Truly You are King of kings and Lord of lords. You were the innocent Lamb that was slain for my sins. Jesus, You are the great Mediator. Your Name is above all names, and one day every knee will bow and every tongue will confess that You are Lord. Oh how I love You—You made an Oath, swore by it, and that covenant still stands today. You are not like a man that You would go back on Your Oath, but I can depend on Your Word. I'm no longer Pressed like I used to be. I lift my hands to You, oh Lord, for You have done marvelous things! My spirit has been Quieted like a child being rocked to sleep in his mother's arms.

My **Redeemer**, oh how I adore You. You **Sacrificed** Your-self and emerged **Triumphant**. Thank You for Your **Unfailing** love. Thank You for being a **Giver**. My **Vision** is no longer blurred. You give joy, peace, mercy, and wisdom, and I **Worship** You. To say that You are **X**-tra large is an insult because You're bigger than life, **Yahweh**. Thank You for being the covenant-keeping God. If **Zion** can sing because You dwell in the midst of it, so will I sing of Your goodness because You're in my midst as well.

Yes, God is all of the above and more. That's why we have to expand our praise. He's too big—we must stretch ourselves when it comes to praising Him.

Here's another warm-up using familiar biblical terms. Remember, though, as we get further, we'll branch out into the nontraditional praise. But it will all glorify God. Your praise will take you to higher levels. No longer will your praise be repetitive and mundane because you don't have anything else to say; you'll branch out and give God your best. Get ready to put your praise on . . .

Father, I praise You because You are **Almighty** God. There is no other God but You. Thank You for the **Blood** shed by Your Son Jesus on the **Cross** at Calvary that I might be free from sin, sickness, and spiritual death. I praise You for the **Covenant** that I have with You, one that has been in place since my great, great, great . . . grandfather Abraham. You swore by it then and it still applies to me now. You have always been my **Deliverer**, setting me free from the traps that the enemy set for me, and when I listen to You, You keep me from ever stepping into those traps.

You're my Example of how I should live and have given me Your Word. You have been a Faithful Father, One I can depend on in every situation, One who has never Failed me. I will Glorify Your Name forevermore. You have given me the most precious Gift anyone could ever have in the Person of Holy Spirit, Who is a Friend and comfort to me. I am Insatiable, I can't get enough of You! Thank You for being Jehovah God. I can call on You anytime I need You because You are the One who's always there. There are no Kinks in Your plan! Your Leadership is impeccable. Not only are You a Merciful God, but You're the Most High God!

Thank You Lord, that my Name is written in the "Lamb's book of life." Your ears are always Open to hear me when I call. You Promised You would never leave nor forsake me—and in this I have confidence. When I think about all that You are, my mind becomes Quiet and I can again Rest and know that I'm Safe in Your arms.

Thank You for being my Teacher, Holy Spirit. You guide me into all Truth, helping me to Understand You and Your Love for me. My lips shall Utter praise, as I learn from Thy statutes, which help me live free from sin. I Vow to love and Worship You all the days of my life.

You are the X that causes blessings to be multiplied in my life. You, oh God, are my everything! I would be a big fat Zero without You!

When you begin to praise God like this, you will see that because all of your efforts are used in thinking about Who He is and what you're going to say, your mind can't wander on to other things. Thus, you get lost in ministering to God!

By the way, I only found one English word that began with *X* in the King James Bible. It refers to Ahasuerus, who was a king God used to save the Jews. Therefore, we must be creative and use other words that can be described by *X* such as "multiply."

STRICTLY FROM THE HEART

I will praise thee, O Lord, with my whole heart; I will shew forth all thy marvelous works.

PSALM 9:1

Sometimes you want to just pour out your heart to God. You'll have one of those days, especially when people disappoint you and God comes through, where you know that if not for Him, you wouldn't know what to do. You'll find yourself with such a feeling of gratitude and thanksgiving that all you want to do is tell God how much you love and care for Him. When you feel like that, one letter won't do. You will use double, triple, and quadruple letters of the alphabet.

The ABC's of Praise is like a bridge that will connect you to God *right away.* This particular praise is just what the title says: strictly from the heart. I want you to read it first, then reflect on your day. If it applies, once again after you read it, lift your hands and verbalize it to the Lord. If you want to change anything, or if Holy Spirit brings something to mind, remember this is your book. Get a pen or pencil and insert what's in your heart. Then give God some praise.

Lord—today I want to express from my heart how much You mean to me. It amazes me how You Always Arrange Your time around mine. Never could I accuse You of being an Absent God. Thank You for being Actively involved in my life. You never, ever tell me You are too Busy to talk with me. It Boggles the mind. After all, You are the God who created the heavens and earth. You're magnificent, yet You're always there for me. Even when I Babble about what's Bothering me, You never Brush me off or tell me to "get to the point!" You are Capable of handling my problems and those in China at the same time. I'm so Comfortable around You. Your love Carries me when I'm weak and beat-up. You are a Colossal God. I can Depend on You even when I know that I've wronged someone, including You. You're so worthy of praise. How can I withhold it from You! I won't, I can't. You're so special to me.

You've caused broken Dreams to come to pass. Disappointments that I never thought I could recover from, You've found a way to Ease my pain. Your Ear is always open to hear my cry. How Excellent are You, oh God!

If only I would learn to seek You first before I take on projects—things would be much Easier. You've said You would lead and guide me and every time I've sought You, never once have You gone back on Your Word. What a God of integrity You are!

Faithful Father, how much Fairer can You be? Your Word says to seek You First, in the morning and evening. You're so Generous with Your blessings. Your Gentle voice wakes me every morning. I have sense enough to know that it is not the alarm clock. You Give me bread to eat. You provide spiritual, physical, and financial Growth in my life. When I ask, You provide Guidance and even when I don't, Your Grace sustains me, and You still lead me in the right direction. I would be out of my mind to not praise such a worthy God!

I have a Home, thanks to You. You've provided Heat in the winter. You've broken Habits and caused me to be joint Heir with You.

You've never been Icy with me. Your warmth is so Inviting. I never Imagined that it could be this good between us. You have never Isolated Yourself from me, which causes my Journey to be so much easier. I've never had to Jump through hoops to be with You. I'm Joined with You forever, and that makes me feel so secure.

Jesus, thank You for being my High Priest and going to the Father on my behalf. You're too good to me!

You have Kept me. Your Kindness goes beyond anything I can imagine. I never have to worry about You Kicking me to the curb. You'll never give up on me because of Your Love. Lessons Learned in the past sometimes are still hindrances keeping me from my today, preventing me from getting to my tomorrow. How can I forget the Messes I've gotten myself into—You've Managed to get me out of them all, even though I know I'm still responsible for what I've done. You are right in the Middle, telling me I can make it. You and I are a Majority, what comfort.

I have Someone on my side who is not afraid of anything, and that Someone is You, oh Lord. Before our relationship, I thought I knew what I could and couldn't live without. I've found out that the one thing Necessary in my life is You. Nothing is too hard or difficult for You. I no longer have to be beat up. Nay, in all things I am a conqueror.

Overwhelmed—only when I neglect to focus on You! My Opportunities to walk in Your blessings have increased. Your Word has caused my eyes to Open and see Your goodness. You, oh God, have Peeled away doubt and fear. Nobody but You Picked me up when I was so low I thought I could not make it. Bless the Name of the Lord—You are marvelous! You have become the Problem Solver in my life. I never Question Your commitment to me. Before I really came to know You, I was a Quitter. Now, I've become a fighter, and thanks to You I win. You've caused critics to be Quieted. You've Restored Relationships and things that mean so much to me. I must admit that there are times in my life where You are the only Reason I can Rise out of bed. You help me Recover when the world says I'm going under. I am Safe in Your arms. I am Strengthened by Your presence. I am Steady in my walk. I praise You for being my Strong Tower—I can run to You and find Safety. Oh how I adore You!

You've set this thing up so that I can Talk to You whenever I please, and I'm grateful for it. With Your help I've Torn down strongholds, my skin has become Thick—words that other people say don't hurt as much because of You. I'm no longer Terrified of what the devil can do because You Travel with me everywhere I go. With You on my side—what can man do to me?

Any praise I render to You is Understated because of Your greatness. I don't Understand all there is to You but this I know, You do love me, You do care for me, You do protect me,

You do provide for me. You cause me to have the Upper hand in every situation. Uncommon is Your love and I'm glad that You loved me first. Oh yeah, You Volunteered to love me—nobody forced You or paid You, it was a Voluntary act. You saw me in my sinful state and still chose me.

Only after I tried in Vain, You filled that Vacant spot that no other could fill. You told me from Your Word how Valuable I was. My Vision is no longer blurred; I know who I am thanks to You.

You are Wonderful. You are marvelous. Thank You for Washing me and making me clean. Thank You for taking my Weaknesses and turning them into strengths. Thank You for Working with me. Thank You for not abandoning me!

Nobody can cross me out by putting an X through my name because of You! When folks close one door, You open another. Your X-ray eyes can see my heart, You know me and yet You still love me—glory to Your Name forever!

You are the Holy One! You are the One I Yearn for. You are the Yoke destroyer. You keep me from being an emotional Yo-Yo—up one day and down another. Uncertain about my future—NO! I can be steady because of You. How can I be so confident—because I'm Yours—I belong to You and You are well able to take care of what's Yours.

I Zip through life because of You. I don't walk through life like a Zombie with no hope. I'm alive, I'm alive, I'm alive because of You—thank You, Lord, You are miraculous and *I love You!*

Selah!

Praising from the Valley

By him therefore let us offer the sacrifice of praise to God continually, that is, the fruit of our lips giving thanks to his name.

Hebrews 13:15

Most of this book was written *not* when I was on the mountaintop but when I was in the valley! Even though we tend to focus on the negatives in our life, praising God will lift us high above any situation or circumstance.

On payday, we may pay all of our bills except two. Then we focus on the two we didn't pay. The next time you find that happening, praise God for the bills that were paid and thank Him that the other two will be.

If you have six kids and all are serving God but two, the enemy will have you focus on the two who are not. Give a shout of praise for the four, and thank Him that the other two will serve Him as well. You need to remember that your worst day is a good day in the life of someone else! There are many people who would trade lives with you any day.

This next praise was written on Wednesday, August 13, 2003, at 9:35 p.m. I still had the seventy-two cents in my pocket from the previous Monday. That summer for me was a rough time. The Lord instructed me to work for the school system so I could write during the summer, but I would be remiss if I didn't tell you that I was disobedient most of the time. Something always vied for my time, and, sad to say, I yielded to the demands and never did much writing. Because of my disobedience, I didn't prosper, but it was no one's fault but my own. God still provided, even in my disobedience, but I could have been further along financially had I been writing as He instructed me to.

It was near the end of the summer when I finally admitted to God that I was sorry for the days I had secretly pouted. I knew I enjoyed many days of sweet fellowship with the Lord, so I thanked Him that, despite my empty pockets, I was still rich beyond measure. I was healthy, I enjoyed a nice home. I had a great family—not perfect but great. However, I didn't hide the fact that I didn't enjoy not having money in my pocket to indulge in pleasures I had become accustomed to.

I had vowed that I was not going to ask anyone for anything anymore. If God didn't do it, I would go without. It was hard. There were many people I could have called on the phone and said, "I have seventy-two cents in my pocket, can you give me twenty dollars?" And they probably would have given me more. But I was determined not to beg (yes, I said *beg*) anyone for money.

That night at church I ran into several people and my flesh was yelling, "Tell them! Tell them! You're almost out of gas and you have seventy-two cents in your pocket." But I refused to yield.

I listened to the Word, then left church with a smile on my face. Everyone I met asked, "How you doing, girl?" or "Hey, what's going on?" My flesh wanted to say, "I have seventy-two cents in my pocket and I need some money!" but I didn't. I smiled and said, "Things are great," and I left and went home. Even though I lacked many of the things I desired, I was determined to show a love and appreciation for the Lord that wouldn't even allow me to feel depressed. Praise is not something you do when everything is going great and you feel like it. Our Heavenly Father is so wonderful and so good to us that even if you only have seventy-two cents you should not withhold praise. Praise isn't tied to God's pocketbook! Praise is attached to our love for Him and His love for us!

When I got home from church that evening, I really wanted to tune into the Golf Channel. The final PGA Major was going on and I wanted to see how Tiger Woods was doing. My body didn't want to write, especially about "praise," because I didn't *f e e l* like "praising." But in my heart, I knew I should. I had a mandate from the Lord, and after all, I was only writing what I had been practicing myself, so why should I tire? I was judging my praise by my circumstance and, in reality, my circumstance didn't have anything to do with whether I praised God or not.

Holy Spirit gently reminded me that Tiger Woods—and everyone else on that show—had their millions. Some of them perhaps didn't know or even acknowledge that there was a God. I only knew I had an opportunity to praise the Lord and I was considering choosing Tiger Woods over Him. Determined that my God deserved my obedience, I decided to pen a praise. Sometimes we all need to sit down and think about praise, especially during difficult times.

Like me, you may choose to write your praise, but don't stop there. After you write your praise, put down the paper and raise your hands and open your mouth and speak forth the things that come from your heart. Think about where you are right now and how you feel. Emotions will run the gamut. Some of you are very satisfied and happy. Some of you are in a state of euphoria or utopia. And some of you feel lonely, depressed, and helpless. No matter what state you are in emotionally, the Lord is with you. You can be alone but you don't have to be lonely. Things in your life could have regressed, but you don't have to be depressed. Remember, you don't have to feel helpless, you have a Helper.

Read this praise and then I want you to write one based on how you feel at this moment:

Father, I come to You this evening, thanking You for things in my life that You've done over the years. I refuse to dwell on this moment and all of the things I lack. You're so wonderful, I'm not going to Allow my current situation to dictate that I withhold praise from You. Belief in You has Carried me. I honor You with my mouth and with my thoughts. Determined to Erase all the negatives that I Face, I proclaim my love for You and I thank You for Gently Holding me in Your arms.

I can feel Your Irresistible pull. Judging my surroundings do me no good. But Keeping my thoughts on You and Loving You in spite of what I feel means more to me at this moment than Money in my pocket or any Need I may think I have. If I were honest, the things I long for aren't necessities. There is truly no One like You. There are no friends I can call who can satisfy me like You. Oh, to think what life would be without You. My Opposition would have a field day! A mess it would be. Just praising You tonight has Propelled me out of my present circumstances. I needed something to get me out of the

Quagmire I'm in and Rise above it. That something is You. I am Sustained by Your love.

Truthfully, I never thought that our relationship would ever get to this. I now Understand what my grandmother and saints of old meant when they sang "What a Friend We Have in Jesus." I refuse to forfeit my peace. No—You paid much too great a price—You paid with Your life. I Vow to not let anything come between us. Just You Wait and see, I'll love You forever. I've found out by living this thing that love X love = more love. I feel Youthful in Your presence—Young and in love. Your love times my love equals a life filled with love, how could I lose?

Yes, I sit here and pen from my heart my feelings. No longer am I thinking or concentrating on the things I thought so important an hour ago. I'm just basking in this moment with You. Though the enemy tried to steal my joy—once again my Zeal has been exposed. The smile on my face says it all. I'm in love with a very Special Person. My Lord, how good You are!

No TV program, no phone call from a friend, no flavor of ice cream could have pulled me from where I was over an hour ago to where I am now. I thank You with all of my heart—and I'm loving You more each day.

Your daughter, Gloria!

Folks, I can't begin to tell you how I felt after writing that praise. No money, no man, no friend could bring such joy. As soon as I finished writing, I raised my hands in praise and spoke what I just wrote to the Lord.

Every word of that praise came from my heart. I didn't have to use the dictionary, because the flow was there. I believe my overflow came from the reservoir that I've built up. You'll get that way too. There will be times when using the dictionary will be an option, but, as you get proficient in the ABC's of Praise, you'll be so full that you'll just flow. You'll get "lost in His presence." I most certainly did.

JEHOVAH JIREH—OUR PROVIDER

I will praise thee, O Lord my God, with all my heart: and I will glorify thy name for evermore.

PSALM 86:12

L ife has a way of teaching us that "we're not all that." You begin to realize the only One who is constant with His provision is God. When you've maxed out your credit cards, the 401(k) is gone, and the ATM machine scowls and says, "Don't even try it," you realize that if God does not step in, you're going under.

When you're between a rock and a hard place, give a praise to Jehovah Jireh—your Provider. Come with hands lifted up—let's give Him His due:

Father, this is an Awful situation I'm facing. It seems as though I'm getting Beat down on every hand. However, I was reminded today that You're still here. You are and will always be Jehovah Jireh my Provider.

My Circumstance has changed, but my Covenant with You has not. You *will* Deliver me out of this situation. I Expect victory because You are Faithful. You are God and do not change. You are my present Help. I am no longer Immature about Who You are. I know that I can depend on You. So Joyfully I proclaim that I have a Keen awareness of my past victories and my future in You. I am no longer spiritually dull. I will not Lay down and give up because I win. Why? Because I have You.

I Manage my emotions and I do not Neglect my confession of faith. Because I'm Obedient and confess what You say about me, Positive things will begin to happen. The enemy can no longer Quell my confidence. I know how to enter into Your Rest. Thank You, Lord, for being my Provider.

See, You've done it again, Suddenly, I no longer feel Trapped. I am Unmoved by what I see. Vague are those things that weighed me down before I entered into Your presence. I can now Wait patiently for my deliverance.

Lord, do You realize what effect You have on people? Being in Your presence one minute can change a life. I know that I can make it! Nobody can talk me out of it! Your love has just covered me with a blanket of peace. Thank You! Thank You! Thank You!

I no longer feel broke down, but refreshed. Jesus, You are the XO [Executive Officer] in charge of my affairs. I thank You that the spirit of heaviness is far from me. No matter how loud the enemy Yaks [babble, chatter], my confession of who You are causes him to Zip it up! Satan has to be quiet because You are the greater One and Holy Spirit lives in me. Yes, I am an overcomer! Thank You, Jehovah Jireh, for being my Provider.

KEEP PRAISING—YOU HAVE HIS EAR

Every day will I bless thee; and I will praise thy name for ever and ever.

PSALM 145:2

This particular praise is one to thank God for His *accessibility*. You don't need to stand in line and take a number, He's always there for you. If you really thought about this statement, it should leave you reeling. Think what would happen if you wanted to talk to the president of the United States. To some, he is the most important person in the world. If you wanted an appointment just to sit down and talk with him—fat chance.

But the God who created the universe; His Son, Jesus, Who gave His life for you; and Holy Spirit will talk to you at any time. Doesn't that just blow your mind?

I was thinking about all this one day and the following praise flowed from my lips. You may not feel this one, but write your own. This one will let you know how I feel.

Father, I want to praise and thank You for being Accessible to me. You're so easy to Approach. Your lovingkindness is present even when I miss it. Thank You for helping me to bring Balance into my life—that mental stability I need. The Confidence I have in You will never Cease to exist because there is no end in You. I thank You for my grandparents and parents who never Debated Your existence. They never quarreled or questioned You, which allowed me to grow up knowing You did Exist indeed! I thank You that I've always been Free to call on the Name of the Lord. Until today, I never really realized the wonderful Gift my parents instilled in me as a Girl—that You were a real Person to be respected and Honored. While I've always paid Homage to You, for many years, I was Ignorant of Who You were, and how much Your Son Jesus had to pay for me. As a little girl I watched grown-ups throw their hands in the air to praise You; I thought they were Kooks—eccentric, strange people. But now I realize they had something more precious than I could even imagine. Love makes you strange to those who haven't yet experienced love—especially being in Love with You.

You're Majestic; a royal, Magnificent God who brightens the heart and lifts the heads of those whose countenance has been darkened by the things of the world. Never could I ever foresee how much You would mean to me and be a part of my life. My Objective is to infect as many people as possible with Your wonderful love. Personally, I'm surprised myself at the effect You have on me. I refuse to Quarrel with individuals while trying to defend Your existence. Why get involved in an angry dispute with ill-informed people?

The facts all point to You. Life has a way of Removing the Scales that blind unbelief. Sooner or later Truth prevails and they will have an Urgency to Understand why those who love and cherish You feel like we do. Until then—their hearts will be Vacant, empty, Void of the love that can only be filled by You.

What a Waste to live life without You. It's impossible to be Whole unless You're an intricate part of one's life.

I'm just so thankful that each day I wake up You're mine and I don't have to share my time alone with You with anyone! Yielding to You was the smartest decision I've ever made. You're X-tra large in my life and You belong to me! Thank You for the constant Zest in our relationship. I enjoy and love You with all my heart!

See, you have to think about this kind of praise, it doesn't just roll off your lips. You must spend some time—but it's worth it!

LET NOTHING BLOCK YOU FROM LOVING GOD

The Lord is my strength and my shield; my heart trusted in him, and I am helped: therefore my heart greatly rejoiceth; and with my song will I praise him.

PSALM 28:7

Once you develop a relationship with God, you will become increasingly more conscious of His goodness and character. Your heart will become even more tender. You'll find yourself holding your hands up as you go through the house saying "Lord, thank You, Father, I just love You so much!" And when you love someone, it's *e-a-s-y* to give praise. Conversely, if you're angry or mad, it's difficult. I have three children and two grandchildren. I constantly shower praises on them. When they're in my presence, praise rolls off my tongue because of our relationship. When I'm angry with them, and yes there are times when the relationship is challenged, there is not much praise coming from my lips.

When I was a babe in the Lord, I didn't give praise. I wasn't taught to praise Him, and frankly, I had some issues with God that kept me from praising Him.

My mom died when she was fifty-seven, and I was still very young in the Lord. I loved my mom very much. She was sweet, easygoing, and very lovable. While I never verbalized my feelings to God, I blamed Him for letting her die. After all, He was God, He could do anything; why didn't He save my mom? Well, little did I know at the time that the person to blame wasn't God. If we read our Bible, and back then I was reading everything but my Bible, God gives us some clear directions on how we treat our "temples/bodies." We have only one body and if we abuse it, it will give out on us.

God also tells us to pray for one another. Once I began to read the Bible for myself, I realized that my mother played a part in leaving early, and I, as her daughter, didn't do my part either. Yes, I was ignorant of prayer and how to pray, but ignorance is no excuse and it has its price. When I saw behavior contrary to the Word of God in my mother's life, I didn't pray. When my mom was in the hospital, my prayers weren't faith filled or laced with the Word. I feel I could have done something to help if I had only known how—but I didn't.

Then, my dad, who I loved with all my heart, came to live with me when he was about sixty-four years old. At the time he was an alcoholic. I must be honest and tell you that I did not want my father to come live with me for that reason alone. And I thought it would be the excuse that would release me from having him come. I don't drink, but Holy Spirit knows how to get your attention in such a Gentlemanly way. While I was focusing on my dad's drinking, Holy Spirit reminded me that I was a chocoholic (chocolate lover) and chickaholic (fried chicken lover), and at the time I didn't have control over either. My chocolate called me like my dad's alcohol called him. Whereas my dad drank in abundance the first of the month after receiving his check, I cooked fried chicken in abundance every week I got paid. When I began to look at myself and all the things I needed to control, I no longer judged my dad.

As Christians, we sometimes forget our struggles and we focus too much on what we perceive is sin in others. The Word says in Matthew 7:3–5: *"And why beholdest thou the mote that is in thy brother's eye, but considerest not the beam that is in thine own eye? Or how wilt thou say to thy brother, Let me pull out the mote out of thine eye; and behold, a beam is in thine own eye? Thou Hypocrite, first cast out the beam out of thine own eye; and then shalt thou see clearly to cast out the mote out of thy brother's eye."* When God tells you to do something, don't try to wiggle out of it by telling Him what another person is doing wrong. He didn't ask me for excuses. He gave me a directive, and my approach to wanting Dad delivered from alcoholism should have been different. My love should have been the driving force instead of judgment. It was easy for me to see Dad's sins because I had taken my eyes off mine. God wanted my dad delivered, but He wanted me delivered as well.

God does not want us to become experts at judging others. Instead, He wants us to be diligent at judging ourselves. Matthew 7:1–2 reads: *"Judge not, that ye be not judged. For with what judgment ye judge, ye shall be judged: and with what measure ye mete, it shall be measured to you again."* I was looking for excuses. But God dealt with my heart and I'm so glad He did.

Because my dad came to live with me, *after* I received years of "teaching," and "Bible reading," my prayers for him were Word based and effective. My kids and I would lay hands on my dad and pray for him. Our prayers, along with those of my brothers and sisters and others, made a difference. Because of spiritual growth—history did not repeat itself.

Even before my dad moved in with me, I constantly covered him with prayer, something I didn't do for my mom . . . I prayed that even in his foolishness (drinking until he passed out), that the angels of the Lord would protect him and keep him from danger. I prayed that people would not take advantage of him while he was in a drunken stupor. I prayed that God would preserve him.

A week before my dad came to live with me, I told him, "Dad, you know I don't drink and I don't allow drinking in my home. If you come to live with me, you must promise that you won't drink." My dad's reply: "Baby, I will quit—Daddy won't drink."

Now, under normal circumstances I wouldn't have even thought about believing him, because he had promised many, many times before that he was going to quit, only to take another drink. The difference in his promise to me, however, was the fact that I had prayed for deliverance and I knew that God not only hears but He would answer my prayer.

Dad lived with me for seven years until he went to be with the Lord at seventy-two. And he never drank in my house. I can count a few times in that seven-year stretch when some of his friends picked him up and brought him back drunk; however, after my brief and candid conversation with them—when I in no uncertain terms told them to "never let that happen again"—I didn't have to deal with the alcohol anymore.

What was the difference in my mom and dad? Prayer. There were other issues, but the lack of prayer on my part was one. You may say, "And what does this have to do with praise?" During my mother's illness and a couple of years after her death, I came to grips with the truth that God wasn't responsible.

I could not praise God even if I knew how back then, because I blamed Him for my mom's death. How can you praise someone who let your mom die? How could I tell God how wonderful He is when I thought He was responsible for my mom's death? How can you lift your hands and proclaim that a Person is the greatest when you think He turned His back on you during one of the most critical times in your life?

If you're harboring negative feelings about God, you won't praise Him. If you're mad at God and you believe He's part of the problem and not the solution—you won't praise Him. But I've come to set you free if you want freedom. God didn't do it! No matter what someone told you, or no matter if all evidence points toward Him—trust me—He is innocent and He didn't cause your sorrow.

John 10:10–11 says: *"The thief* [satan] *cometh not, but for to steal, and to kill, and to destroy: I am come that they* [us] *might have life, and that they might have it more abundantly. I am the good shepherd: the good shepherd giveth his life for the sheep."*

We do have a real enemy, but it is not God. Why would Someone give His Son so we could be saved if He was the bad guy? Why would Jesus die on the cross if His Father wanted to "make us pay"? Why would Jesus give us Holy Spirit to lead, guide, and direct us if God wanted to "get us"?

You need to get over being angry with God. Get rid of any blame so that you can boldly raise your hands in praise to the God who so deserves it! If you're withholding your praise because you blame God for something—repent (1 John 1:9). Tell God you're sorry and pray Luke 12:2. Ask God to reveal to you what happened to cause your anger, then believe and request that God send someone across your path who will help you find answers. Then begin to read your Bible.

I prayed the following prayer for all of you who might harbor anger in your hearts as I wrote this book. Read this prayer and open your heart to receive a breakthrough.

Dear Heavenly Father, I come to You on behalf of the person reading this book who may have an issue of the heart.

They need Divine intervention on Your behalf. Provide answers, wisdom, revelation, and healing as only You can. Father, send laborers across their paths that will help them to see how wonderful You are and people who will help them find answers to the concerns they have. Father, help them find a church that will provide godly counsel from the Word of God. Grow them up spiritually so that once they're delivered, they will help others who are in need. Thank You, Father, that those who once hurt, hurt no more. Thank You for healing them and setting them free in the Name of Jesus I pray—Amen.

I know God answers my prayers and He will answer yours. Receive your deliverance and, as an act of your faith, thank God now for the load that has been lifted from your shoulders.

Now that you're free, never pass up an opportunity to praise. When you feel it, say it! When you don't feel like it, say it! I don't care where you are or how "silly" you may feel. Only the devil will try to make you feel ridiculous when it comes to praise. But trust me—God is smiling and that's all that counts. If you're at a formal dinner I'm not telling you to jump up with your tuxedo on and holler "Glory to God!" Just look up while everyone else is talking about their achievements and say under your breath, "God even at this boring formal dinner, I see and feel Your love and I just want to thank You."

As you lie in bed tonight, instead of saying your regular prayer, try mixing your prayer with praise using the ABC's of Praise. You can do half of the alphabet tonight and think of the other half for tomorrow. Perhaps it will go something like this:

Father, as I lie here in the bed You've blessed me with, I just want to tell You how grateful I am to You for all You've done.

In spite of my day, You've seen to it that I'm **Alert**, **Bathed** and **Comfortable** in a bed that You've provided for me. As I listened to the news and saw that **Danger** was all around, none came nigh my dwelling.

I lie here **Excited** at Your Word in Psalm 4:8 that says: *"I will both lay me down in peace, and sleep: for thou, Lord, only makest me dwell in safety."* That tells me You knew that I'd be living in this neighborhood a long time ago, and You still said I would "dwell in safety." You also said in Proverbs 3:24 that *"When thou liest down, thou shalt not be afraid: yea, thou shalt lie down, and thy sleep shall be sweet."* So I will not be **Fearful**. Thank You, Father, for Your protection and sweet sleep.

You've blessed me with **Food** to eat, I'm **Gifted** with Your presence. As I laid down tonight and when I awake in the morning, my **Friend**, precious Holy Spirit, will be here with me. If I face anything, **Help** is not on the way, it's **Here** with me. You're my **Incentive** for getting out of bed tomorrow. I also thank You that as I **Juggled** the many assignments I had today, it was You who caused me to have victory. Thank You, Lord, for my **Kinfolk**, continue to save those who are in need of You. I give You praise for Your protection over them today and ask for continued blessings on tomorrow. Bless them with the desires that line up with Your Word. May they, too, lift holy hands to praise You.

When I get up in the morning, I'll honor You by walking in **Love**, and last but not least—may I never forget how magnificent You are, in Jesus' Name—Amen.

Now isn't that better than "Now I lay me down to sleep . . ."

PRAISE WHEN YOU'RE NAUGHTY

I will call upon the Lord, who is worthy to be praised: so shall I be saved from mine enemies.

PSALM 18:3

We must recognize that God deserves praise in every situation. There are several definitions of praise, one being "the expression of gratitude for personal favors conferred." Praise can't get any more personal than when we *know* we've done something real dumb and *didn't* get what we deserved.

Let's not forget that when we praise God, we are telling Him thanks for the many things He has done for us. Praising Him, especially in difficult circumstances, helps us forget our problems and realize that we have a Friend who is always willing to comfort us. That's why I wanted to show you how you can praise God for the "naughty" things you've done, the stupid moves you've made, and the danger from which He rescued you. If you were out in the world and someone rescued you, you would thank them or bestow accolades upon them. Then why not do that much more for God? He deserves our praise, too.

Come to know God for being in the middle of everything you do. And praise Him for everything. Consider this scenario: You've had a bad day and did not act or respond to some situation as you should have—you've been naughty instead of nice. When that happens, you can do one of two things: You can beat yourself up, or you can slip over into praise. The benefit of the ABC's of Praise is that you must force your mind to get in sync with your spirit. Make yourself start with a word that begins with *A* and go all the way to *Z*, thinking about how God intervened and how you're going to give Him praise.

First, recall the situation. Raise your hands when you think about what *could* have happened. Then start your praise . . .

Absolutely, Father, I am Ashamed of the way I Acted today. But as always, You Brought me out of my Crisis. My Circle of so-called friends Couldn't even restrain me. You, however, Delivered me before I could Destroy my testimony. Did I Deserve the mercy? No. Did I Deserve the grace? No. But You saw fit to once again Extend to me Your kindness. I see clearly now what happens when we are Eager to take matters into our own hands instead of doing things Your way.

The Enemy set a perfect trap for me today. Eyes wide open, I Fell into it. No, it was not Your Fault, because Your Word has taught me over and over to Forgive. But I chose this day to *react*. I let my Guard down, Gave into the pressure. But You Holy Spirit helped me Gather my thoughts so that I could get a Handle on the situation. Oh the Hazard of yielding to the flesh. I stand before You now, Honoring You. I can't Ignore

Your power when I yield to it. God, Imagine what would have happened if I had continued to Ignore Holy Spirit. The Image of what could have happened is frightening, to say the least. My faith and all that I represent would have been the Joke of the office. I was in Jeopardy of losing my testimony.

I Kneel before You, Lord. You deserve all the Kudos. Thank You once again for saving me from myself. What Lessons I have Learned . . . Leave situations when you know they are escalating. Labor to do the right thing. The Lack of Your Word is detrimental to my Legacy in You. Lord, my Mission is to please You, I've made Many Mistakes before; today was no exception. But thanks to You my spiritual Muscles are becoming well developed, becoming defined in the things of God, and Maturing, thanks to Holy Spirit.

Nay, I am more than a conquerer, because I've come to know that I Need this time with You to express my appreciation. To some, I'm just a Number, but to You, I'm a daughter who is cherished and loved. Never have I Needed You more than Now to Nurse the wounds that life inflicts on us all. Your sweet Oil of gladness is so soothing. It just pays to Obey You. Thank You for being my Oasis, thank You for taking away the Pain.

How can I Pay You for all You've done? You're the only Person I know who forgives and forgets, once I confess my sin to You. I can bring anything to You. You've never told me my issues were too Petty. You never Pick and choose the sins You'll forgive. When I come to You asking forgiveness, You forgive all. I'm so thankful. You are Quite something! Simply remarkable!

My constant Refuge, my Relief and Reason for existing. Refresh me, Holy Spirit. Strengthen me, Sustain me where I'm weak—I *can* be Strong because of You. Continue to Teach, Train, and Take me to levels I never knew I could reach. Uncover areas in my life that are Unholy and Unhealthy, areas I can change with the help of Holy Spirit.

Victory belongs to me. Virtue is mine. Nothing is Void in my life. Thank You for Washing me in Your blood. Thank You, Jesus, for Winning the War. Thank You for Your Wonderful presence, Holy Spirit. You are large, no, You're better than large, You're X-tra large in my life.

I Yearn to be more like You, Jesus, and in my Yearning, sometimes I just have to Yawl [cry out] because of Your patience with me. Yea, Your company is sweet. I'll be passionate in my pursuit of Your Word. May my Zeal never wane [it won't diminish, decrease, or decline]. Like Zeri in 1 Chronicles 25:3, I shall continue to *praise You at all times*, even when I act *stupid!*

When you do this, you've embraced God's love even in the difficult times. As a result, you don't continue to beat yourself up. You move on quicker and you've become vulnerable to the One Who loves you more than anyone else in the world!

It took me some time to write this praise because I had to think about this scenario and get the dictionary. You might need to do the same. But you will have spent the time praising God.

Often we are so lazy. We are satisfied using the same words and expressions over and over, but God wants us to branch out. He wants us to increase our vocabulary when we talk to Him. When we do that, we will be able to better express to Him how we feel. As you build your vocabulary praising God, you'll express yourself better in your everyday life!

Can't you see the Father's face when you admit, "God You're too big, I'm at a loss for what I want to say. But telling You how I feel is really important to me right now, so bear with me, Father, I'm going to the dictionary. I'm going to dig and search and look until I find the words to express Who You are and how I feel about You right now because You mean that much to me"?

Our Heavenly Father is looking at you with His chest sticking out because He's thinking, "They could have given up and turned on the TV, but it means that much to them, that they are willing to go to the dictionary to express their love to Me! What, you say!"

Others Who Praised

Bless the Lord, O my soul: and all that is within me, bless his holy name.

PSALM 103:1

There are many examples in the Bible of people who offered up praise to God, and their praise wasn't limited to the times when everything was going well for them.

Leah was the first wife of Jacob, not by choice, but by default. Her story is told in Genesis, chapters 29 to 35. Leah was a woman who, through trickery, found herself married to a man who was more in love with her sister Rachel. Leah lived her life in the shadow of her younger sister, competing for her husband's love. She even thought that by having Jacob's children she would win the love she wanted so badly. It didn't work then and it won't work now.

Four boys later, Leah finally saw the light. She named her fourth son Judah, and, instead of thinking about her husband, she thought about God and realized God loved her. He had seen her tears and had shown her favor by opening her womb and blessing her with children. In Genesis 29:35 she forgot about her husband and herself and said, "Now will I praise the Lord." Later she bore more children, but she never won the place in her husband's heart for which she yearned.

Many of us look for love in all the wrong places. The world would make us feel unloved and unappreciated, but God loved us so much that He gave His only Son, proving His love for us. While others reject us, God has always and will always love us. We should always direct our energy and bless the Lord with our praise. Praise Him for His love.

Has God blessed you with children? Praise Him for your children. They may not be everything you want them to be, but we haven't been perfect parents either. If you begin to praise God for your children, you'll see things change. It's a blessing from God to have an open, fertile womb. Don't even think it's because you're all that, it's because God has blessed you and He deserves praise.

If you haven't had children yet and you and your husband desire them, pray for your womb to open in the Name of Jesus and start giving God praise for your children, and watch that womb open up. Speak faith daily and then send me a praise report later.

Deborah was a military leader, prophet, judge, and wife. Her story is told in Judges, chapters 4 and 5. Deborah was in leadership when it was unusual for a woman to be in a position of authority. Her example shows you that when God appoints you, it doesn't matter what the norm may be at that particular time—no one will be able to stop your promotion.

After winning a great battle, instead of touting what a great military leader she was, Deborah chose to sing praises to God. It would have been very easy for her to credit her smarts and wisdom, reminding the people "it took a woman to do this." But Deborah was smarter than that. She gave credit to the One who deserved it. Deborah and Barak sang praises in chapter 5, verse 2, of Judges.

What victories or accomplishments have you patted yourself on the back for, neglecting to praise God? Has God won any battles for you lately? Has He gotten you out of any messes? Has He avenged you like he avenged Israel? Like Deborah and Barak, give God some praise. Now would be a good time to lift your hands and thank Him.

Deborah also served as a judge who settled disputes. Has God been your judge and settled some legal affairs and personal arguments? Lift those hands again and praise Him.

David was a shepherd, warrior, and king. His story is told in 1 Samuel, chapter 16 through 1 Kings 2. David, as we know, was a great king who had some great mess ups as well. However, he loved God. At the end of his life, David wanted to rebuild the temple for God, but God told him through the prophet Nathan (2 Samuel 7:1–13 and 1 Kings 8:17–19) that his seed (Solomon) would build the temple. David, however, wanted to make sure that his son was successful in this endeavor, so he began to put in place strategies to ensure the success of the temple's construction.

David's story continues in 1 Chronicles 23:1–30. He gathered all Israel's leaders, men at least thirty years of age, and gave them assignments. In the midst of assigning officials, judges, and supervisors, David assigned four thousand men to praise the Lord by playing musical instruments David had given them. But he didn't stop there. Whenever he made assignments for specific duties, David also called this group to give thanks and praise to God every morning and evening. Wow! Some leaders would view this as a waste of manpower—not David. He constantly reminded those he ruled that God's ever-present help in their lives deserved praise. I believe that's one of the reasons for David's success. Psalms, which is divided into Divisions, is also filled with praises from David.

Are you a leader who emphasizes praise to God for what He's done in your life? Amidst the everyday finagling to get the job done, does God get the praise He deserves for your success? If you were moved from your position tomorrow, would people know that praise was a part of your legacy? Perhaps you don't have the manpower or authority to assign praisers, but you can be one. I know that many of you are already, but what about the rest of you? Give God praise for your company.

Paul and Silas sang loud praises while in jail (Acts 16:25).

Zacharias was struck dumb for months, yet when his tongue was loosed, and he could finally talk, his first words were praises to Almighty God (Luke 1:64).

Look up others in the Bible who were in difficult situations but chose to praise rather than pout. Be one of them.

THE BOOK OF PRAISE: PSALMS

For the Lord is great, and greatly to be praised: he is to be feared above all gods.

PSALM 96:4

The book of Psalms is filled with praise. Within each Division there are stanzas where you should spend some time and allow God's Spirit to minister to you about praise. It takes approximately four hours (give or take) to read the entire book of Psalms, not meditate on them, but only to read them. What a perfect way to spend an evening or weekend afternoon!

While you're reading Psalms, circle, star, or highlight Scripture that talks about praise. Then commit some of the Scripture to memory so you can confess them out of your mouth.

Let me just share an example from my own life of why praise is so important. While working in a suburban high school, I noticed that when students came into the office, more often than not, they were rude, obnoxious, and noisy; their attitude demanded that you stopped what you were doing *now* to solve their problems, which were critical to them. Each child acted as if they were the only kid in school.

Children behave that way. Most of them are only concerned with their issues and, the majority of the time, their issues are not issues at all. But to these kids they were mountains that needed to be moved ASAP. If we gently corrected their attitude or approach, they'd storm out of student services, mumbling and yelling expletives. This went on day after day. Believe it or not—many of the parents acted the same way.

Then, once in a blue moon, there were those kids who would come in and say, "Hi, I just came in to see you and tell you to have a good day." We wanted to jump over the counter and hug them. Of course we couldn't, but just hearing a friendly voice bearing glad tidings was like a breath of fresh air. When students did this, I would find a way to bless them.

As I thought about these students, Holy Spirit said to me, "How do you think God feels? Every day millions of His children, from different backgrounds, come into His presence. Some are rude, others sulk, and their attitude demands that God fix their problems, which they deem critical. Some, like the high school kids, don't even say 'hello' to God—they just spout off their concerns and issues, not even thinking once about God and His feelings."

Imagine people worldwide asking, begging, blaming, crying, and speaking unbelief and you can envision how our Father feels. Can you picture how God feels when one of His children comes in and says, "God how was Your day? Have I told You lately how much I adore You? Do You realize You are the reason I choose to live?" How many of you just come into His presence stretching your arms out saying how blessed you are to have a Dad like Him?

If God can get jealous, and Jesus can cry, They can also hurt when we fail to offer due praise. We need to continually honor God. Let me give you Scripture for what I just said. In Exodus 20:5; 34:14; Deuteronomy 4:24; 5:9; 6:15; Joshua 24:19; and Nahum 1:2 Scripture refers to God's being jealous of anything that's put before Him. One verse even says that His name is "jealous." John 11:35 says, "Jesus wept." Here Jesus was in the midst of friends who were hurting and weeping because Lazarus had died. Seeing all the pain, He wept as well. If He didn't have feelings He wouldn't have cried.

When we act like we care about God and we're not ashamed to show Him love and affection, there is nothing God won't do for us. Promise yourself to be God's child who will give Him glory and honor. Let God know that you appreciate Him. When He hears your voice it should be music to His ears. His chest should swell as He says—"listen to My child—his words are like music to My ears." Remember the scripture in 1 Corinthians 2:9: *"But as it is written, Eye hath not seen, nor ear heard, neither have entered into the heart of man, the things which God hath prepared for them that love him."*

God has proven His faithfulness to us over and over again. Let's be faithful in our praise to Him. It doesn't cost anything but the yielding of our tongue.

One Labor Day, my children (who are all grown) were not around. I was by myself—but not alone. I decided the day before to cook outside so that I could have a quiet day to write (I am beginning to see that it is not only a gift, but a passion). I got up praising God, but not with my usual ABC's. Instead, I decided to be Spirit led.

I proceeded to tidy up, prepare my clothes for the week and wash clothes, all the while focusing on and giving thanks to the Lord. I put on a Christian video (teaching tape) while folding clothes and gave praises as the minister poured out truths from God's Word that were truths in my life as well.

Then it was time to wash, press, and curl my hair (that's a praise report in and of itself). I turned off the video and put on a CD. As the lyrics bellowed praises, I found myself putting down the straightening comb and curlers, making a decision that praise was more important. I could do my hair later.

When my mind began to wander, I did what the Word said and quoted God's promises. Sometime during that day I said my ABC's of Praise. Satan kept trying to bring ugly thoughts to me, but I quoted Scripture from my friend David in the Bible, which said, *"Thy words have I hid in my heart that I might not sin against you."* Those ugly thoughts left as fast as they tried to come.

Sometimes when you are alone, the enemy will try to fill your mind with thoughts that are ungodly, but praise acts like a shield that will help you keep the darts from connecting.

When I completed my to-do list, it was 6:00 p.m. I sat down to write. Before typing a word, however, I was acutely aware of a wonderful peace. I felt like a person who didn't have a care in the world. I reflected that I had been smiling all day, enjoying the company of Someone I love dearly.

When you find yourself alone, turn off the TV. Don't look for the phone book to call someone. Take the opportunity to praise all day. Having a day of thanking God and praising Him is sweet.

Maybe you'll choose to go through the Bible and find scriptures on praise or just sit and read the book of Psalms. Maybe like me, you'll just want to praise out of your overflow. Continued praise will take you places you've never been.

Each section of this book begins with Scripture that talks about praise. Here are a few more references for you from Psalms: Psalm 9:2, 11, 14; 18:49; 21:13; 22:3, 22, 23; 34:1; 35:28; 44:8; 45:17; 47:6; 48:1; 50:23; 56:4; 57:7; 66:8; 67:3; 68:32; 69:30, 34; 71:6, 14; 74:21;

75:9; 79:13; 92:1; 96:2, 4; 98:4; 102:18; 106:1, 48; 107:8 (This exact stanza is repeated several more times, 107:15, 21, and 31); 108:1, 3; 109:1, 30; 111:1; 112:1; 113:1, 3, 9; 115:12, 18; 116:19; 118:19, 21; 119:7, 164, 171, 175; 134:1; 135:1, 21; 138:1; 139:14; 144:9; 145:4, 10, 21; 146:1; 147:7, 12; 148:1–5, 7, 13; 149:1, 3, 6; 150:1–5. Read them, highlight them, and commit some to memory.

Don't Quit—Keep Praising

Praise ye the Lord: for it is good to sing praises unto our God; for it is pleasant; and praise is comely.

PSALM 147:1

I'm going to challenge you to never quit growing in your praise toward God. Perhaps one day, you'll write a book to help people go even higher. I want you to use this section to write two more praises. Use doubles or triples. Write a song or a poem, but write two praises. It may take you a couple of days, but you can do it. Listen to Holy Spirit because He knows what's in your heart and He'll help you write it.

Do you remember the twenty-six things I wrote to help you achieve your desire to "raise your praise and get lost in Him"? Refer back to that section and re-read the confession. You'll be encouraged.

Praise 1: Write your words first.

A   =   _____

B   =   _____

C = _____

D = _____

E = _____

F = _____

G = _____

H = _____

I = _____

J = _____

K = _____

L = _____

M = _____

N = _____

O = _____

P = _____

Q = _____

R = _____

S = _____

T = _____

U = _____

V = _____

W = _____

X = _____

Y = _____

Z = _____

Now write your praise from the words you've penned above:

_____

_____

_____

_____

_____

_____

_____

_____

_____

_____

_____

_____

_____

_____

_____

Praise 2: Write your words first.

A = _____

B = _____

C = _____

D = _____

E = _____

F = _____

G = _____

H = _____

I = _____

J = _____

K = _____

L = _____

M = _____

N = _____

O = _____

P = _____

Q = _____

R = _____

S = _____

T = _____

U = _____

V = _____

W = _____

X = _____

Y = _____

Z = _____

Now write your praise from the words you've penned above:

_____

_____

_____

_____

_____

_____

_____

_____

_____

_____

_____

_____

_____

_____

_____

I'm sure that if your experience is anything like mine, you're grinning from ear to ear.

USE SCRIPTURE AS YOUR ABC'S OF PRAISE

Thou art my God, and I will praise thee: thou art my God, I will exalt thee.

PSALM 118:28

This particular praise is written using Scripture. I really like this one because it's God's Word.

Father, thank You for Your **A**ngels You've given charge over me so that I won't even dash my foot against a stone. —Psalm 91:11

Lord I will **B**less You today and every day. Praises of You will continually flow from my mouth. —Psalm 34:1

Jesus, You died for me so that I could **C**lobber the enemy. I am a **C**onqueror through You! Thanks for all You've done. —Romans 8:37

Father, I have been Delivered from Darkness because of Your Son and I'm grateful. —Colossians 1:13

Father, I thank You for giving me Eternal life as Your child. —John 3:15

Thank You, Father, for not showing Favoritism. You love me as much as You love anyone else. —Romans 2:11

Lord, You are Great and Greatly to be praised. —Psalm 48:1

I thank You, Lord, that I don't have to fear men because You are my Helper. Who can come against me and win?—nobody! —Hebrews 13:6

Father, You made me in Your Image—a copy of You. I know some good people, but there is no one on earth I'd rather be a replica of other than You. Oh how I worship You. —Genesis 1:27

Father, You are not just my Joy but You're my exceeding joy. Your Joy is above and beyond anything I can imagine. When the world says I should be sad, that exceeding joy kicks in. When all is not going well, that exceeding Joy bubbles up in my soul. Thank You for Your Joy that's greater than anything I could imagine. —Psalm 43:4

Jesus, You are such the Gentleman. You stand at the door and Knock when You could have flexed Your finger or kicked the door in. Thank You for not leaving and allowing me to come to my senses and open the door to You and all that You give. You have never forced anything on me. That's another reason why I love You so much. —Revelation 3:20

You promised me that no one could come between our Love—nothing—never. I can't be separated from You by life, power, principality, or even death! You are truly an awesome God. —Romans 8:35

Father, great and Marvelous are Thy works, great and Marvelous are Thy works! —Revelation 15:3

Father, Your Name alone makes the devil tremble and You have given me the authority to use that Name and ask the Father anything—what a privilege, what an honor. Thank You for trusting me with such a precious Name.
—James 2:19; John 16:23

I am a world Overcomer and I got that way by believing in You—What perks. Thank You, Lord! —1 John 5:4–5

You are my Preserver who keeps me from trouble, what a caring God You are. —Psalm 32:7

Father, thank You for Your Quick Word that's alive and full of power. Because Your Word is Quick—and alive—I speak Your Word and things happen! —Hebrews 4:12

You are my Redeemer who keeps me from destruction; nobody and nothing can do that but You and I honor You! —Psalm 103:4

You are the Satisfier who fills my mouth with good things. —Psalm 103:5

Lord, You are the great Transformer who turns me into Your likeness. —2 Corinthians 3:18

Thank You for dying for the Ungodly—that was me before I accepted You. —Romans 5:6

Father, because I'm Your sheep, I know Your Voice and I hear You—You are not obscure to me. I will follow You, and as I follow Your Voice—no one can pluck me out of Your hands. I will flee from the stranger's voice and I will not follow him. I love You, my Shepherd. —John 10: 4–5, 27–28

Father, because I'm Your **Workmanship**, I don't have to feel inferior to anyone. Thank You for my self-esteem that cannot be taken away. —Ephesians 2:10

Lord, "**X**" represents multiplication and You've promised in Your Word to multiply my seeds that I sow, so that I can increase. You could have just "added" my seeds, but no, You're the God of too much, You've got multiplication on Your mind and I am so honored and grateful for what You do for me. —2 Corinthians 9:10

Because of You, my **Youth** is renewed as the eagle—what love! —Psalm 103:5

Thank You, Lord, I am **Zealous** of Your laws because they keep me out of trouble. —Acts 2:20

It's time for another praise exercise. I want you to research Scripture and use the following pages to write your praise. It may take a while to complete the praise because you will start with the letter *A* and go to *Z*. When you finish, lift your hands and voice your praise. Remember, find the Scripture, write the praise in a sentence, and don't forget to record the Scripture reference.

Begin to write your Scripture praise:

_____

_____

_____

_____

_____

_____

LIFT UP YOUR HANDS

_____

_____

_____

_____

_____

_____

_____

_____

_____

_____

_____

_____

_____

_____

_____

_____

_____

_____

_____

_____

_____

_____

_____

_____

_____

_____

_____

_____

_____

_____

_____

_____

_____

_____

Praise Filled with Thanksgiving

Offer unto God thanksgiving; and pay thy vows unto the most High: And call upon me in the day of trouble: I will deliver thee, and thou shalt glorify me.

PSALM 50:14–15

There are many reasons why we give thanks, but we often forget to be thankful for some of the things we take for granted.

You need to be careful when you allow yourself to slip into that "woe is me" funk. The Bible has something to say about people who are not thankful. For example, Romans 1:21–22 says: *"Because that, when they knew God, they glorified him not as God, neither were thankful; but became vain in their imaginations, and their foolish heart was darkened. Professing themselves to be wise, they became foolish."*

You are a foolish person when you become thankless—when you begin to say "What do I have to be thankful for?" Read the following praise, then read it again substituting your own words.

Nothing I can do or say will cause You to Abandon me! Wow!

You're so faithful.

I thank You, Lord, for Believing in me and allowing me the opportunity to enjoy life. I thank You for Cradling me in Your arms when I needed Your Comfort.

Father, thank You for the Detailed way in which You created each one of us. We were so important to You that no one person has the same fingerprint out of the billions of people on earth. Even our teeth are unique. You didn't compare or copy us, You chose to create originals, because our worth meant that much to You. When You made one, You threw away the mold.

You blessed us with various Emotions that only You could have placed within us. You allowed us to feel the wonderfulness of love. We can share laughter. We know that we can overcome hurts and disappointments. Yes, even when we fail, we experience the anticipation and excitement of trying again. Why? Because we know we will experience the thrill of victory! You put that winning spirit on the inside of us.

Thank You for allowing us to Feel the warmth of a hug. The passion of a kiss. A father and a mother's love. Not to mention the excitement at the birth of a child and to witness that child's innocence.

And Father, thank You for putting a little extra something in Grandchildren. What joy we receive just looking at them. You didn't have to do that, but You did.

We have Houses to protect us from the elements. We have Hope because of You. Thank You for not judging us on our Ignorance, blaming You for disasters and personal calamities. You told us in John 10:10 that it is the enemy who comes to steal, kill, and destroy. Jesus, You came so that we could have life and have it more abundantly.

Jesus, what a gift You are! You were minding Your own business when God Your Father asked You to give up everything to come and save us—what love.

Your Kindness is everlasting in Your mercy shown toward me, how can I thank You enough. I am so indebted to You.

Thank You for being a Lifetime Partner. After I accepted You and Your love, Your commitment to stand by me was sealed forever in heaven.

Thank You for the Meticulous way in which You created the earth with such variety and beauty. The timeliness of each season fills us with awe: summer's breeze, which blows ever so gently; fall's breathless colors; winter's snow, which paints a beautiful white blanket; and spring's wonderful smell of rain and flowers in bloom. The wonder of a new sunrise is as intoxicating as the view of a full moon. The ocean waves dance and stars wink at us. We behold the various flowers, the assortment of trees, and plants in all shapes and sizes. Beauty is all around us. I thank You for this and more.

You Nursed me back to health when I was spiritually and physically sick. You made sure that there was no Obstruction between You, Your Son, and Holy Spirit as it relates to me. I don't need a third-party to reach You.

My chest swells with Pride when I think of how much You love me. It's because of Your love that I don't have to Quake when I miss it. You have given me the authority to cleanse myself with Your Word.

Lord, Your Reputation has stood the test of time. It cannot be copied or surpassed. Thank You for Saturating us with Your presence. There is no place we can go where You are not! What comfort! I Treasure You more than anything! You Trust me when I can't trust myself.

Thank You for being Unselfish. You could have decided to let things be just You Three. But that's the kind of God You are, always thinking about me.

You could have left the earth Void, but You chose to have fellowship with us; it boggles the mind. You Watch over us daily and I'm so grateful for that. X marks the spot in my heart reserved for You and You alone. No one or nothing can fill that spot but You.

You never Yell when we make mistakes. You quietly speak to us via Holy Spirit. I'm glad You don't yell because we would probably disintegrate (smile). Thank You for taking care of me. I would have Zonked out by now had it not been for You!

Each time I read this praise, I find myself adding more to it. We are all blessed beyond belief. Stop the pity party! Give thanks.

POTPOURRI PRAISE

If ye abide in me, and my words abide in you, ye shall ask what ye will, and it shall be done unto you.

JOHN 15:7

. . . in which it was impossible for God to lie, . . .

HEBREWS 6:18

As I was completing this book I asked God: "What are some of the things I've forgotten to praise You for?" In His infinite wisdom He reminded me of some things.

I began thinking about those things we tend to forget or wish to sweep under the rug. Before I continue, let me remind you that earlier I talked about being fake—not being honest. So I must be honest and confess that I'm running out of *X, Y,* and *Z* words! If you see them omitted in any of the following praises, you add them!

The next eight praises represent what God gave me when I asked the question: "What did I forget that You want in this book?" I was reminded of so many things—that's why this first one is titled "Potpourri Praise." It has a little of everything in it.

These praises are so individual that I want you to pen a praise after each one. I know you'll be thinking of things that pertain to your life as you read them. Don't forget to read the praise first, then prop the book up and lift your hands and speak the praise from your heart again. I know the Lord will be pleased as you think and write about His goodness. When you're ready, lift your hands and say, "Father I praise You for . . ."

My **A**uthority in the earth; my **B**usinesses; my **C**hildren and my **C**hildren's Children; I praise You for granting me some of my **D**esires.

I praise You that when I use my authority my **E**nemies are defeated; I praise You for my **F**amily; my **G**uardian angels. I praise You for making me the **H**ead and not the tail. I praise You for my **I**nheritance of eternal life [Matthew 19:29 and 25:34]; I can't praise You enough for **J**esus, oh how I love that Name; Jesus, wonderful Savior, Jesus, soon and coming **K**ing.

Thank You for Your promise that says You will never **L**eave me. I praise You for being **M**aster—Ruler of all. I praise You because I'm not just a **N**umber to You, I'm special. Lord, You don't **O**ccasionally [now and then] think of me, I'm always on Your mind and I love You for it! Thank You for **P**ursuing me.

I **Q**uiver just thinking about Your greatness and the impact it has had on my life. I praise You for being the **R**emarkable God that You are and for making me a **S**uccess, for **T**eaching me how to love, for **U**ttering things to me by Holy Spirit that I would have otherwise never known. I praise You for being my **V**isionary and **W**hetting my appetite for Your Word and the way You do things. I **Y**ield my tongue and praise You!

I believe the Lord is pleased, but I just feel a song is what we need right now. Go ahead, sing Him a song from your heart. Pick any song that comes to mind. If you can't think of anything, try "What a Friend We Have in Jesus"—that one always works—or make up one yourself. He's not picky when it comes to praise—just honored.

Write your words first.

A = _____

B = _____

C = _____

D = _____

E = _____

F = _____

G = _____

H = _____

I = _____

J = _____

K = _____

L = _____

M = _____

N = _____

O = _____

P = _____

Q = _____

R = _____

S = _____

T = _____

U = _____

V = _____

W = _____

X = _____

Y = _____

Z = _____

Now write your praise from the words you've penned above:

_____

_____

_____

_____

_____

_____

_____

_____

_____

_____

_____

_____

_____

_____

_____

_____

_____

_____

_____

_____

_____

PRAISE GOD FOR COURAGE

I can do all things through Christ which strengtheneth me.

PHILIPPIANS 4:13

Do you know that you can do anything you put your mind to? Sure you can. If you answered no to my question, this praise will bless you. Knowing you can do something is half the battle in tackling anything. No you can't do it by yourself, but with Jesus you can. What's been difficult for you? Let's tackle that thing with praise. All you need to do is add the Word of God, listen to what He tells you (remember, His voice is that whisper you hear, what you think is *your* intuition), and the outcome will be nothing short of miraculous.

Before we begin, picture that thing you wish to do but just don't have the courage to step out and do yet. Did you picture it? Do you believe God is in it and it's His desire for you to do it? Then let's praise.

Father, today I want to thank You for being my Answer to this thing I didn't have the courage to attempt. You are my answer to the Bully who has tried to keep me bound. I will now Charge forward because no longer will I be Damaged by my past and all the "can't do" thoughts. I praise You and I will no longer be Embarrassed but Effective, not Frightened but Fearless, no longer Gawky but Graceful. I will not be Hindered or Harassed; instead, I'll Hasten to do what You've said because my Help is here—ready to make easy the task! Glory to Your Name! How can I praise You with such confidence? Because You said that I could do it *and I will!*

You've Ignited a fire in me and I thank You! I praise You for Jolting me out of the state I was in by giving me a Holy Ghost Kick. Oh it worked! Thank You, Lord. Thank You for removing Layers of doubt and lifting my Morale. No one can Navigate a life like You, and I honor You. Obstacles will now be seen as Opportunities for You to use someone else to help me get this thing done! Pow! Another black eye for the devil. Oh how I praise You! Lord, You are Quite something. My Refuge, my Support, my Teammate. Together we can Undertake anything! I praise You that I'm no longer a Victim but a Victor. Thank You for Waking me up! Your plan has my Wholehearted attention. I love You and I know that I'll never be the same. Thank You for Yanking me from my slumber so that I can reach my potential. I will no longer ZigZag through life, I can be bold and just walk the straight and narrow. Thank You for helping me see that this thing will be done. I praise You for my courage. You're good, marvelous, and wonderful. Hallelujah to Your Name!

The lack of courage in your life can have devastating effects for you and those who come in contact with you. Now that you have your courage back—never give into pressure again.

Write your words first.

A = _____

B = _____

C = _____

D = _____

E = _____

F = _____

G = _____

H = _____

I = _____

J = _____

K = _____

L = _____

M = _____

N = _____

O = _____

P = _____

Q = _____

R = _____

S = _____

T = _____

U = _____

V = _____

W = _____

X = _____

Y = _____

Z = _____

Now write your praise from the words you've penned above:

_____

_____

_____

_____

_____

_____

_____

_____

_____

_____

_____

_____

_____

Praise God for Your Future

For I know the thoughts that I think toward you, says the Lord, thoughts of peace and not of evil, to give you a future and a hope.

Jeremiah 29:11 (NKJV)

Now that you know (or were reminded) in the last chapter that you can do anything and you've given God praise for the thing you thought you couldn't do—there's more. Yes, God is the energizer—He keeps going, and going, and going because there is so much to do. You have a bright future, not because I said it but because of God's Word. You may not know what the future holds but God does, so let's praise God for our future.

Father You are an **Amazing** God and I honor You this day. I can let **Bygones** be **Bygones** [forgetting the problems of the past]. Lord, for so long I tried to do things my way, but I'm going to honor You by letting You be in Charge of my life. You're my Choice to lead and guide me. When I make Decisions about my life and I factor in You, I can do more than I ever thought I could do. Father, I praise You because only You can give someone their "Dream job" with no Experience. I praise You for giving me Holy Spirit who is the great Encourager. Thank You for helping me Focus.

Goals are reachable because of You. I praise You for the opportunity of being Your child. Just knowing You Love me and knowing that You'll never give up on me has had a Huge impact on my life. I'm no longer Insecure about the future. When I get in a Jam, You're there to help me. Thank You, Father, I'm no longer a Killjoy [complainer, pessimist, worrywart], I have hope.

I praise You for taking the fear out of Learning. I praise You for Motivating me. Thank You for Your Word that Navigates my future. I can Openly discuss anything with You. I love You because it's never too late to change my Profession because of You. Thank You for causing things to happen Quicker than normal.

Relying on You gives me a peace no one else can give. Even when the world says I should Retire, You tell me to Re-fire into something new. I'm so Secure in You. I give You praise for elevating my Thought life. Father, I praise You for making me Unique. I don't have to try to be like someone else. Doing that would only cause me to miss out on what You've called me to do. Thank You for being a Voice in my future. I can speak forth the blessings of God because You have my back.

Lord, thank You for not holding against me all the Wrong choices in my life. You are the God who takes nothing and makes something out of it. I love You more with each passing day.

I get up looking ahead. Yeah! Yeah! You be the Man, Lord. Yeah! You be the Man! And because You are the Man, I thank You that I don't have to read Zodiac signs to determine my future. You've already told me what Your desire is in the scriptures. I just need to be obedient because You've already provided a way for my success. Thank You, Lord. I praise You for all that You've done!

Wow, this praise is *real*, folks, and you should be jumping for joy about your future. Be a witness to others. Let them know they don't need to call the psychic hotline! Tell them instead to call on the Lord. It amazes me when people worship the stars and ignore the One who created them!

Write your words first.

A = _____

B = _____

C = _____

D = _____

E = _____

F = _____

G = _____

H = _____

I = _____

J = _____

K = _____

L = _____

M = _____

N = _____

O = _____

P = _____

Q = _____

R = _____

S = _____

T = _____

U = _____

V = _____

W = _____

X = _____

Y = _____

Z = _____

Now write your praise from the words you've penned above:

_____

_____

_____

_____

_____

_____

_____

_____

_____

_____

_____

_____

_____

_____

_____

_____

Don't Allow One Day to Spoil Your Remaining Years

This is the day which the Lord has made; we will rejoice and be glad in it.

PSALM 118:24

Every day you open your eyes is a blessed day, and that's why I was compelled to write the next praise. It may prove to be very controversial but I don't mean it to be. It's a praise about a horrific day in history—September 11, 2001.

Innocent people were killed and others forever scarred mentally (only because they don't know Jesus), and I'm not making light of it. It was a horrible time for our nation. I cried and prayed along with many. But it seems to me that some people do not want to look ahead. They want to remain in the past and they want to keep you with them.

Think about this: Do you believe that God wants you to spend every September 11 from now on reliving the pain? I don't think so.

He wants you free. I believe if you will get up on that day and start it with praise, the presence of Almighty God will cover you like a warm blanket in a blizzard. Your praise will set the tone for that day and you will emerge stronger and more fulfilled as a result of your praise.

Determine that you are not going to allow the enemy to control you on September 11, but you are going to make a decision on purpose to have fun and enjoy the day. No, we can't erase the past, but we can skip into the future. Let's praise.

Father, I will not feel Awkward today about being happy. I will not. You've been too good to me and this nation. I praise You for a Breakthrough this day. I call on the Comforter, precious Holy Spirit to move in and out of the hearts of those who lost loved ones. I will not let others Define this day for me. I will praise and Embrace You today. With Your help, I will keep my Emotions in check. I will help others see Your goodness. I praise You for Your Faithfulness, oh God, for removing Hurts.

I will be Immovable in my faith and Ignore the urge to follow the world. This day will not be Jinxed but blessed. This nation will be free from any terrorist attacks. I praise You for being the Keeper of this nation. We will experience Laughter this day. Gone are the broken hearts, gone be the pain. Father, I praise You for being a Magnet that draws others to You by Your Love. Nurture them as never before.

I will think of You Often today. It is the only way I can be assured of success and Peace. I stand in the gap right now for those who are in a Quandary today. I praise You for moving on their behalf to bring solutions right now. Remind them by Your Spirit that when pillows were Soggy with Tears, it was the finger of God that wiped away those Tears.

I honor You because our future is not Uncertain. We are Victors, Warriors, there is no Yellow streak down our backs. We are Zealots [enthusiasts] for You and we choose to start this day like any other—with praise and thanksgiving!

Make sure you pray for someone else every September 11. When you see planes in the air, pray for the safety of all who are aboard. Keep the pilots and staff in prayer, especially the personnel in air traffic control. Pray that they are alert and watchful. It doesn't matter whether you know anyone who works for the airlines—they still need our prayers.

Write your words first.

A = _____

B = _____

C = _____

D = _____

E = _____

F = _____

G = _____

H = _____

I = _____

J = _____

K = _____

L = _____

M = _____

N = _____

O = _____

P = _____

Q = _____

R = _____

S = _____

T = _____

U = _____

V = _____

W = _____

X = _____

Y = _____

Z = _____

Now write your praise from the words you've penned above:

_____

_____

_____

_____

_____

_____

_____

_____

_____

_____

_____

_____

_____

_____

_____

_____

PRAISE GOD FOR THE UNITED STATES OF AMERICA

Blessed is the nation whose God is the Lord; and the people whom he hath chosen for his own inheritance.

PSALM 33:12

That last praise reminded me of just how blessed we are in the United States. This nation was built on godly principles and I feel we should praise God for our nation. You may ask, "Why praise God for the United States?" Do you read the papers? Hello, we're at war. Have you checked out the homeless situation lately?

See, that's the kind of negative thinking you must stop. Focus instead on the good and speak blessings over our nation. No, the United States isn't perfect. You know why? I live in the United States. And if all of the millions of people were perfect but me, it still wouldn't be a perfect place because I live here. What about you? Are you perfect? So that makes two imperfect people living in the United States. In order for something to be perfect, *every thing* associated with that thing must be perfect.

We're praising God for all the wonderful things that are good about our country. And there are many. There's no other place I'd rather live. Sometimes I find myself singing "God Bless America." When you sing that song, believe it or not, you're speaking blessings over your nation in song and God is pleased. If you haven't read 1 Timothy 2:1–8 recently, read it. We're admonished to pray for people in authority. Why? So we can live a quiet and peaceful life. If you're not praying, then don't complain about the state of our country. Yes, I am aware that all people are not free like those who live in the United States. That's why we need to continue to pray for other countries so they, too, will be free. We should not be satisfied until all nations are. So join me and praise God for the United States.

Father, thank You for blessing America and the Banks that secure our currency. I give You praise for Corporations that provide well-paying jobs. I praise You for such a Developed and productive nation. Thank You for a healthy Economy and the opportunity for Education. I praise You for Families who have the freedom to live in harmony with each other without being separated.

I praise You for Governments that protect American people at home and abroad. I praise You for the High standard of living we enjoy compared with other nations. I praise You for Investment opportunities and for Judges who monitor the judicial system. I praise You for Kinsmen who pray for this nation and support the United States as allies. I praise You for Laws that govern our land. I thank You that our nation is a Melting pot for all people.

Our Nation is blessed because of You! **Opportunities** are in abundance because of You. Thank You for our **President** who is elected by the people. I give You praise because we can own our own **Property** and because everything does not belong to the state. I praise You for the various **Quotas** and how they have helped bring balance to situations that would be otherwise off balance. I give You praise for **Restrictions** on certain foods that would cause harm to our bodies. I give You praise for **Schools** of learning for just about anything. I thank You for **Tariffs** and **Trade**, which help the economy and our system at large. I praise You for the **Undaunted** spirit of the United States. I thank You for our ability to **Vote**. Thank You for the Veterans who have died in past **Wars** protecting this land. I praise You that even in times of **War**, You provide an army to fight for our rights and the rights of others. No, Father, our nation is not perfect, but we give You praise for it anyway and we want to thank You for blessing, protecting, and providing for the United States of America. I praise You for protecting us in **Years** past and for future years, in Jesus' Name we give You the praise!

When you're home, sing the national anthem in your car or while you're cleaning; you're proclaiming blessings through song. I love America and I am proud to be an American.

Write your words first.

A   =   _____

B   =   _____

C   =   _____

D = _____

E = _____

F = _____

G = _____

H = _____

I = _____

J = _____

K = _____

L = _____

M = _____

N = _____

O = _____

P = _____

Q = _____

R = _____

S = _____

T = _____

U = _____

V = _____

W = _____

X = _____

Y = _____

Z = _____

Now write your praise from the words you've penned above:

_____

_____

_____

_____

_____

_____

_____

_____

_____

_____

_____

_____

_____

_____

_____

I'M FREE AND I LOVE IT!

O praise the Lord, all ye nations: praise him, all ye people.

PSALM 117:1

The scripture above *gives* a mandate for nations to praise God. I know there are millions of people in the United States who praise God. I believe that's why we enjoy our freedom and wealth. After that last praise, I still have some thoughts regarding our freedom.

I don't give God praise often for freedom, so I'm just going to do it now. How about you? Let's praise.

Father, I lift my hands to You today, continuing to thank You for the freedom we enjoy. Thank You for the freedom of Assembly where I can join political parties and fellowship with Believers without worrying about attacks.

I thank You that freedom does not have to be Bought because it's free. Thank You, Father, for moving in the hearts of our country's forefathers to Compose and put in writing the Constitution. Thank You for breaking the Class systems and giving freedom to all. I praise You that I live in a Democratic society where equality and the Dignity of others is recognized. I praise You, oh Lord, for our Economic system, which is responsible in part for the wealth we have. I praise You for Holy Spirit Who acts as a Filter, helping me separate good from evil and truth from lies. Thank You for the Government we have in place that is run *by* the people *for* the people. I thank You for an unselfish nation; we Help other nations in recognizing the good and the bad.

I praise You for raising men and women who have fought for our Independence. I can shout the Name of Jesus and proclaim You as Lord without any repercussions. I have access to Knowledge that would otherwise be hidden from me. I thank You for the due process of Law in which we are innocent until proven guilty. Thank You for the Media. They aren't perfect, but they do provide valuable information we need to coexist with one another. I'm not Naive to think my freedom came without a price; someone paid for it and I praise You. I praise You for this land of Opportunity where I can make a difference. I thank You for freedom of the Press. Though this freedom has many entities, I thank You that we can Publish truths, especially the truth of Your Word. It was this freedom that gave us our Precious Bible and allowed me to write this book.

Thank You for helping me know I don't have to Quake in my boots every time I see the police for fear they'll shoot me because of who I am. In the United States the police are partners. I thank You for the freedom of **Religion**. I can practice my faith without being strong-armed by outside forces. Thank You for **Social** freedom whereby I can speak what I believe. And go where I want to go. Thank You for our armed forces that provide protection when **Threats** appear from our enemies. Thank You, Father, for shielding me from **Unreasonable** men and women who would take advantage of me if they could. Thank You for giving me a **Voice** in government. Thank You for men and women who **Write** godly books to help us grow spiritually.

Father, I thank You. I'll continue to **Yield** to You and vote as You lead. I want to keep the freedom I now enjoy. I will also remember that no matter who wins elections, Father, as godly men and women pray, we can bring about a change. I know, Father, that, without Your intervention, our nation would be little more than a **Zoo** [a group marked by chaos].

Never take your freedom for granted. When you find yourself talking against the United States of America and your freedom, turn on the news or read the paper.

Write your words first.

A   =   _____

B   =   _____

C   =   _____

D   =   _____

E   =   _____

F   =   _____

G = _____

H = _____

I = _____

J = _____

K = _____

L = _____

M = _____

N = _____

O = _____

P = _____

Q = _____

R = _____

S = _____

T = _____

U = _____

V = _____

W = _____

X = _____

Y = _____

Z = _____

Now write your praise from the words you've penned above:

_____

_____

_____

_____

_____

_____

_____

_____

_____

_____

_____

_____

_____

_____

THE EARTH BELONGS TO GOD
BUT WE GET TO ENJOY IT!

While the earth remaineth, seedtime and harvest, and cold and heat, and summer and winter, and day and night shall not cease.

GENESIS 8:22

God never lies! I'm sure that, like me, you've thought of so many things to praise God for besides what I've pointed out. In thinking about our nation, I remembered how blessed we are to go to the store to buy food. I thought about gardens and what they produce. Isn't it amazing that the ground continues to produce, just as God promised?

Let me now speak directly to the pessimist. Yes, I know that we have issues with pesticides and genetically modified foods. Our process is not perfect. You can find a flaw in anything if you look hard enough. But when was the last time you praised God for the very soil that yields our food? Make sure you think about this praise the next time you go to the store. Let's praise God for the earth and the flawless way in which He made it.

Father, I praise You for the Air we breathe. I thank You for the millions of species of Animals, including those who give their lives so our bodies might be nourished. I praise You for the Beaches we enjoy, the Crops that continue to yield us food, and the various Climates. You know it all! You made it all! I praise You for earth's perfect Distance from the sun. Thank You for the Energy sources You supply [natural gas, coal, electricity, oil]. I praise You for the Flawless way in which You created the earth, Farmers who till the ground, Flowers that beautify, Gravitation that keeps us literally on the ground. Thank You for successful Harvests that provide for us year after year and for Your promise of everlasting and abundant life.

Thank You for metals like Iron, copper, silver, and gold that are used to make thousands of products we use daily. But I must pause here and say there is something more valuable and precious than silver and gold—a Jewel named King Jesus—oh yes!

Thank You for all things of the earth: for Lakes that provide an important source of irrigation for farmers and fish for eating, the Moon that lights up the sky in the evening. I praise You for Natural resources [minerals, soils, water, forests and fish]. I praise You for Oceans that dance. I praise You for Plant life—without it there would be no life on earth.

I praise You for the Packaging of our food, which Preserves, Protects, and keeps it fresh for distribution. I thank You for the Quality of our food partly because of the checks and balances we have in place. I praise You for Rich Soil that continues to produce just like You said it would.

I give You praise for the Sun as it rises each morning. I praise You for the warmth and light it provides the earth. I praise You for the wonderful variety of Trees that give oxygen and shade. No one can Undo what You've done and I adore You. Thank You for Vegetables that keep our bodies strong and Water which is a necessity for life. Without it plants, animals, and man could not survive. Thank You because man cannot deplete the Water supply; it keeps recycling itself! You are the *Original Recyclable Guru* and I give You praise. Thank You for the Yucca plants and the metallic element Zinc that is so important to our steel industry.

My head swims when I think about all that You are and this is nothing compared to what You've done. What an awesome God You are! Don't tell me You don't deserve praise! I know better!

Write your words first.

A   =   _____

B   =   _____

C   =   _____

D   =   _____

E   =   _____

F   =   _____

G   =   _____

H   =   _____

I = _____

J = _____

K = _____

L = _____

M = _____

N = _____

O = _____

P = _____

Q = _____

R = _____

S = _____

T = _____

U = _____

V = _____

W = _____

X = _____

Y = _____

Z = _____

Now write your praise from the words you've penned above:

_____

_____

_____

_____

_____

_____

_____

_____

_____

_____

_____

_____

_____

_____

_____

PRAISE FOR INVENTIONS

I wisdom dwell with prudence, and find out knowledge of witty inventions.

PROVERBS 8:12

Our Father has truly blessed us with comforts we would not want to live without. Our lives are easier because of what He's done through obedient people. When I look around my home, my hands rise with praise. What? Take a bath in a tub outside after carrying water from its source and heating it? Not necessary! I love my hot bubble baths. What about indoor plumbing in general, refrigeration, electricity, gas, and central heat and air conditioning? Even if you have only one or two of these modern inventions in your home, you have reason to praise!

This praise reflects what I see as I write. I'm sure that you're going to add your personal praise to this one, so I'm going to leave plenty of room for you to compose your praise(s). Get in the habit of praising

God for everything. Get to the point where a praise is on your lips at all times. *You're going to get to the place in your life where you never complain because you're too busy praising!*

Now that you've got all the fundamentals, I want you to be free to praise using the ABC's any way your imagination takes you. This is a fun praise, so bear with me while I tell you the rules. You don't have to use your ABC's in alphabetical order. You can even leave out some of the letters. I'm suggesting this because we must remember never to put God in a box. If you don't want to do all twenty-six letters of the alphabet—don't. If you want to elaborate more on one particular letter—do so. Do your own thing! You may want to do more than one praise. But remember, I'm going to have some fun praising with this one. God does laugh you know. Here we go:

> Father, as I look around my home and think about where I've been, here are some things I want to praise You for. I know that You use people, but it was You who put the idea on the inside because You were thinking about us. Therefore, I praise You for the following: Appliances that help me with manual labor; Airplanes that take me from one point to the next in record time; Automobiles to travel in; soft Beds that wrap their arms around me and make it hard for me to get up in the mornings(!); Brushes and Combs for my hair; Computers that provide mega information; soft Carpet for the floors; my Church; Clocks to tell time so I won't be late for work; beautiful Dishes; Furnaces to keep the house warm; Food in the Refrigerator; Garbage collectors that come each week. I praise You two times for Garbage collectors.
>
> Father, I just praise You for all Inventions, especially the Iron and Ironing board. Thank You for Lights that enable me

to see and a Switch where just a flip of the finger can turn them on; Money to spend; Makeup; Ovens to bake cakes. Thank You for Pens, Pencils, and Paper to write with; Sofas to lay on to watch Television; Treadmills to hang clothes on—I mean to exercise with; Television so I can watch *I Love Lucy* reruns; Toilets, thank You, Father, for inspiring someone to invent Toilets(!!); Vacuums for the floors; a Washer and Dryer for my clothes; Windows to see Your Creations from; Windows that open to let fresh air into my home. You're just a God of too much and I love You with all my heart!

You know what that praise reminds me of? Picture yourself as a little child with the Lord's face smiling down at you as you stand looking up at Him. You are excited for all He's provided. Then picture Him bending down so He's at your level—His face close to yours. Now, picture your little hands gently pulling His face down so you can plant the longest kiss and declare "I love You, Daddy!"

That's what He wants His people to do! Love Him! Honor Him! The Lord desires a relationship that's pure—one of respect and honor. One that's so special you can call Him Daddy. If you aren't there yet, you will be. Just keep praising and don't forget to fight for your time with Him.

Write your words first.

A   =   _____

B   =   _____

C   =   _____

D   =   _____

E   =   _____

F = _____

G = _____

H = _____

I = _____

J = _____

K = _____

L = _____

M = _____

N = _____

O = _____

P = _____

Q = _____

R = _____

S = _____

T = _____

U = _____

V = _____

W = _____

X = _____

Y = _____

Z = _____

LIFT UP YOUR HANDS

Now write your praise from the words you've penned above:

_____

_____

_____

_____

_____

_____

_____

_____

_____

_____

_____

_____

_____

_____

_____

_____

A Letter of Recommendation

While I live will I praise the Lord: I will sing praises unto my God while I have any being.

PSALM 146:2

Earlier, we talked about how important it is to know God before you can praise appropriately. As I gave this more thought, I did not want to end this book without somehow portraying my love and respect for a Man who's blessed me beyond measure. His credentials stand alone; however, the thought ran across my mind that there may be some of you who still don't really know who this Man is. So I thought I would write a "letter of recommendation" for the Person I'm asking you to get to know. Please understand that this letter of recommendation is not based on what I've heard—but experienced:

August 18, 2004

To Those Who May Not Know:

*It is my sincere desire that you get to know God with your heart and not your head. You see, the One I affectionately call Daddy is **A**vailable to His kids twenty-four-seven, three hundred and sixty-five days a year. He **B**alances His time well and His **B**enefits are off the chart.*

*His **C**haracter is impeccable; His **D**ecision-making skills are the best of the best. He brings **E**nergy to the relationship every day. Your visits never bore Him.*

*He's **F**air in the judgment of others. He provides unlimited **G**rowth to all who call Him Lord. He judges the **H**eart and not your education, income or social status.*

*People all over the world covet His **I**nterpersonal skills and want to be just like Him. You never have to **J**ostle with others for His blessings; He has more than enough for everyone. There is no one on the face of the earth who does not **K**now of Him. However, **K**nowing Him on a personal level should be your priority.*

*This Man is in a **L**eague all by Himself. His **M**anagement style cannot be duplicated because He makes no **M**istakes and does not **N**eglect His duties. **O**blivious to your feelings—never. He does not need a **P**lanner for appointments or **P**ersonal data. He knew you before you were born. Even though He's the Boss who owns everything, He'll be **Q**uiet and allow you to **R**eject His best-laid plans for your life.*

*He won't give up on you. Once you get on target and realize what you've missed, He will **R**estore those things, and He's never said to me once—"I told you so!" His **R**etirement plan cannot be duplicated.*

*His deals are **S**ealed with His Blood, not a pen. He will **T**rain you until you get it right and He performs all of His exit interviews. You always have His **U**ndivided attention. You don't need anyone to **V**alidate your credentials. He gave you every credential you need. He told you that you can do all things through His Son Jesus Christ who strengthens you.*

***W**orkers' compensation is not an option, because this person you're building a relationship with is also a Healer. You can bring all your aches, pains, and scars to Him. Although He's in love with billions of people, when you talk to Him, it's as if you were the only person in the **W**orld.*

*We were nothing, but He proves mathematics to be in the wrong because our nothing **X** [times] His something = everything. Time spent with Him is **Y**ummy. Being accepted as His daughter was the **Z**enith in my life.*

I've given you a heads up. The decision is yours. He has everything to offer and you have everything to gain. Don't be unwise; accept His love and eternal life by accepting Him. You'll be sorry if you don't.

Sincerely,

Gloria P. Pruett,
The King's Daughter

THIS CHAPTER IS EXTRA SPECIAL!

Why art thou cast down, O my soul? And why art thou disquieted in me? Hope thou in God: for I shall yet praise him for the help of his Countenance.

PSALM 42:5

People talk about being in the presence of "movers and shakers." We have the ultimate Movers and Shakers on our side: God the Father, God the Son, and God the Holy Spirit. It can't get *any* better than that! They know how to get any job done.

Our Savior, Jesus, is always there to help us. He petitions the Father on our behalf. Do you know Him as Savior? Is He Lord of your life? If not, He can become your Lord by confessing the following prayer. It is that simple. Don't try to complicate it. The only prerequisite to saying this prayer is that you must mean what you say with your heart. The world will try to tell you that it's more complicated than it is, but trust me, it isn't.

The prayer is based on Romans 10:8–10, which says: *"But what saith it? The word is nigh thee, even in thy mouth, and in thy heart: that is the word of faith, which we preach; That if thou shalt confess with thy mouth the Lord Jesus, and shalt believe in thine heart that God hath raised him from the dead, thou shalt be saved. For with the heart man believeth unto righteousness; and with the mouth confession is made unto salvation."*

If you're sincere about making Jesus Lord over your life, repeat this prayer by saying it out loud so that you can hear yourself. Mean it in your heart and you will be saved right where you are. As I said earlier, don't try to make this complicated, just receive.

> Dear Lord Jesus, I believe that You are the Son of God. I believe that You died on the cross at Calvary, bearing all of my sins for me. They put You in a grave, but I believe that You are no longer there. I believe that You rose from the dead and that You are alive right now. Thank You, Lord, for hearing my prayer. Thank You, Lord, for answering my prayer and coming into my life right now. I believe with my heart and I confess with my mouth that Jesus is now my Lord, Savior, and Master, and as of right now, according to Your Word, "I am born again!"

If you just prayed that prayer, you are now "born again" and your name has been written in the Lamb's Book of Life (Revelation 21:27). When you pass from this world, you will be heaven bound.

Some time ago, the Holy Spirit gave me a psalm for people just like you who prayed this prayer. He wanted you to know how God feels about you now that you've accepted Jesus—His Son—as Lord. Please allow this psalm to minister to you as it did me when Holy Spirit gave it to me.

Lift Up Your Hands

I've been waiting for this day with anticipation you see,
When in your heart you would decide to believe in Me.
Your name is now written in the Lamb's Book of Life.
One day we will be united like a husband and wife.
A home in eternity that's where you'll live—
    It will be your new "hood."
You only get there by accepting Me—not by being "good."
But remember that salvation is just a start.
To develop an intimate relationship would be smart.
Please get to know Holy Spirit, your Earthly Friend,
    Who'll lead and guide you right until the end.
Yes, all the angels in heaven are rejoicing you see,
At the decision you made to confess and accept Me!

By Gloria P. Pruett

CLOSING WORDS

He who brings an offering of praise and thanksgiving honors and glorifies Me: and he who orders his way aright [who prepares the way that I may show him], to him I will demonstrate the salvation of God.

PSALM 50:23 (AMP)

I have been blessed to share with you some of the secrets I use when praising the Lord. As you take your praise to a higher level, take others with you—share the experience of praise.

If you're not attending a church—find one. You need to be around other believers so you can grow and be strengthened. Please know that they are people first, so don't look for perfection. Get into a good Bible teaching church so you can grow in God.

YOU PEN THE END

*Bless the Lord, O my soul. O Lord my God, thou art very great;
thou art clothed with honor and majesty.*

PSALM 104:1

The final pages are reserved for you—yes, you! I want you to write your own ending to this book. I want you to do what I've taught you. Begin to pen words to the Lord. Then, write your praise from the words. Always refer back to previous pages and continue to add on using as many notebooks as you can fill.

Peace to you my brothers and sisters. Know that if I never meet or see you in this life, if you've confessed Jesus as your Lord and Savior, we will meet one day. Until then, keep the pen to the paper. The Lord is waiting—go, write some praises!

—Gloria P. Pruett!

ABC's of Praise

Words, Phrases, or Sentences

A   =   _____

B   =   _____

C   =   _____

D   =   _____

E   =   _____

F   =   _____

G   =   _____

H   =   _____

I   =   _____

J   =   _____

K   =   _____

L   =   _____

M   =   _____

N   =   _____

O   =   _____

P   =   _____

Q   =   _____

R   =   _____

S   =   _____

T   =   _____

U   =   _____

V = _____

W = _____

X = _____

Y = _____

Z = _____

Written Praise Penned from Your Words

_____

_____

_____

_____

_____

_____

_____

_____

_____

_____

_____

_____

_____

_____

_____

_____

ABC's of Praise

Words, Phrases, or Sentences

A = _____

B = _____

C = _____

D = _____

E = _____

F = _____

G = _____

H = _____

I = _____

J = _____

K = _____

L = _____

M = _____

N = _____

O = _____

P = _____

Q = _____

R = _____

S = _____

T   =   _____

U   =   _____

V   =   _____

W   =   _____

X   =   _____

Y   =   _____

Z   =   _____

Written Praise Penned from Your Words

_____

_____

_____

_____

_____

_____

_____

_____

_____

_____

_____

_____

_____

_____

_____

_____

_____

ABC's of Praise

Words, Phrases, or Sentences

A = _____

B = _____

C = _____

D = _____

E = _____

F = _____

G = _____

H = _____

I = _____

J = _____

K = _____

L = _____

M = _____

N = _____

O = _____

P = _____

Q = _____

R = _____

S = _____

T = _____

U = _____

V = _____

W = _____

X = _____

Y = _____

Z = _____

Written Praise Penned from Your Words

_____

_____

_____

_____

_____

_____

_____

_____

_____

_____

_____

_____

_____

_____

_____

_____

ABC's of Praise

Words, Phrases, or Sentences

A   =   _____

B   =   _____

C   =   _____

D   =   _____

E   =   _____

F   =   _____

G   =   _____

H   =   _____

I   =   _____

J   =   _____

K   =   _____

L   =   _____

M   =   _____

N   =   _____

O   =   _____

P = _____

Q = _____

R = _____

S = _____

T = _____

U = _____

V = _____

W = _____

X = _____

Y = _____

Z = _____

Written Praise Penned from Your Words

_____

_____

_____

_____

_____

_____

_____

_____

_____

_____

_____

_____

_____

_____

_____

ABC's of Praise

Words, Phrases, or Sentences

A = _____

B = _____

C = _____

D = _____

E = _____

F = _____

G = _____

H = _____

I = _____

J = _____

K = _____

L = _____

M = _____

N = _____

O = _____

P = _____

Q = _____

R = _____

S = _____

T = _____

U = _____

V = _____

W = _____

X = _____

Y = _____

Z = _____

Written Praise Penned from Your Words

_____

_____

_____

_____

_____

_____

_____

_____

_____

_____

_____

_____

_____

_____

_____

ABC's of Praise

Words, Phrases, or Sentences

A = _____

B = _____

C = _____

D = _____

E = _____

F = _____

G = _____

H = _____

I = _____

J = _____

K = _____

L = _____

M = _____

N = _____

O = _____

P = _____

Q = _____

R = _____

S = _____

T = _____

U = _____

V = _____

W = _____

X = _____

Y = _____

Z = _____

Written Praise Penned from Your Words

_____

_____

_____

_____

_____

ABOUT THE AUTHOR

Gloria P. Pruett is an ordained minister and graduate of the Word of Faith Bible Training Center '96. As a traveling minister, Gloria has preached in various cities across the United States. Prior to her ministerial training, she served on the Praise Team at Word of Faith International Christian Center (WOFICC) for approximately ten years.

Minister Pruett also served for approximately five years at Mitcham Church A.M.E., where she assisted the pastor and headed the singles group. Currently she is fulfilling one of her mandates from God by getting His Word out in written form.

Gloria is the mother of three (Charles, Carlton, and Kelli) and grandmother of two (Carlton II and Cariel). If you were to ask her what motivates her most, she would unequivocally respond "the love of God."

If you are interested in having Minister Pruett speak to your group or congregation, you may write to her at the address below. Or if you just want to mail a praise report, send your correspondence to:

Gloria P. Pruett
P.O. Box 531038
Livonia, MI 48153–1038